SCIENTIFIC SELF-DEFENCE

THE AUTHOR, WITH PROFESSOR OKADA
(Professor of Jui-jitsu, Second Pupil of the Mikado's
Personal Instructor), Shanghai, China, 1908

SCIENTIFIC
SELF-DEFENCE

by

W. E. FAIRBAIRN
Superintendent, Shanghai Municipal Police,
Second Degree Black Belt of Kodokan
Jui-jitsu University, Tokyo, Japan

PROFUSELY ILLUSTRATED

The Official Text Book for the Shanghai
Municipal Police and Hongkong Police

The Naval & Military Press Ltd

Published by

The Naval & Military Press Ltd
Unit 5 Riverside, Brambleside
Bellbrook Industrial Estate
Uckfield, East Sussex
TN22 1QQ England

Tel: +44 (0) 1825 749494

www.naval–military-press.com
www.nmarchive.com

PREFACE

I do not know of any more interesting book to study than *Scientific Self-Defence.*

W. E. Fairbairn, the author, has a most extensive and practical knowledge of this art. I was forced to come to this conclusion when I attempted to grapple with him. Twenty-three years of association with the Shanghai Police Force has given him an experience which he could not get in any other city of the world.

In the early days of the cattle country, the six-shooter was the means of leveling all men to the same size. Now that the sale of the six-shooter is prohibited, every one should have some knowledge of the art of self-defence in cases of emergency.

I take great pleasure in commending this work to every one, and particularly those who have not had the good fortune to be born with great physical strength.

Douglas Fairbanks

FOREWORD

This book is based upon an earlier work issued under the name of *Defendu* which was written for the police forces of the Far East. A second edition of *Defendu* was printed to meet the demand for copies from police and physical directors all over the world.

For this book the title *Scientific Self-Defence* has been selected as it conveys more clearly to the average man the contents of the work. At the same time it should be noted that every method shown in the present work has stood the criticism of police from practically every country in the world, including the Far East, which is the recognized home of jui-jitsu. A more exacting section of the community for criticizing a book on self-defence it would be almost impossible to find.

This system is not to be confounded with Japanese jui-jitsu, Chinese "boxing" or any other known method of defence and although some of the holds, trips, etc., are a combination of several methods, the majority are entirely original and no athletic effort is required to perform any of the exercises given.

After a long experience of methods of attack and defence, I am convinced that no methods that I have seen put into book form meet the requirements of the average man and present-day conditions. It should be realized that in boxing, wrestling and jui-jitsu competitions, etc., the competitors, in addition to having the spirit of fair-play ingrained in them from boyhood, are further protected from foul blows by the presence of a referee, but when dealing with street ruffians, burglars or armed robbers, one is faced by opponents or assailants who will recognize no bounds so long as their objective is attained and they can make good their escape.

The methods of defence explained and illustrated in this book have been specially selected for the man who requires quick knowledge of the best and easiest means of defending himself against almost every form of attack. It teaches a number of admittedly drastic and unpleasant forms of defences but all are justifiable and necessary if one is to protect himself against the foul methods

vii

that are used by a certain class. It further teaches how to protect certain vital parts of the body and it will be noted that the illustrations clearly emphasize this point.

W. E. FAIRBAIRN

Shanghai, China.

NOTE

It should be noted that the author has lived in Shanghai from 1907 to the present date. For years he was the Instructor in Self-Defence to the Shanghai Municipal Police and includes among his pupils, royalty and several of the highest jui-jitsu experts of Japan. He has made a scientific study of practically every known method of self-defence including the following:

Japanese jui-jitsu

For which he holds the Second Degree BLACK BELT of Kodokan Jui-jitsu University, Tokyo, Japan.

The author is the first foreigner living outside of Japan to be awarded a Black Belt Degree by Kodokan Jui-jitsu University.

Chinese "boxing"

Studied under Tsai Ching Tung (now aged 83) who at one time was employed at the Imperial Palace, Peking, as an Instructor to Retainers of the late Dowager Empress.

CONTENTS

xi

CONTENTS

HOLDS THAT ARE EFFECTIVE

HOW TO THROW AN ASSAILANT

USE OF BATON, "NIGHT STICK" OR CLUB

CONTENTS

SCIENTIFIC SELF-DEFENCE

No. 1.—Wrist Hold.

(*a*) Your assailant seizes your right wrist with his left
hand (Fig. 1). To make him release his hold:—Bend your
arm towards your body and turn it in the direction of his
thumb (Fig. 2).

Fig. 1

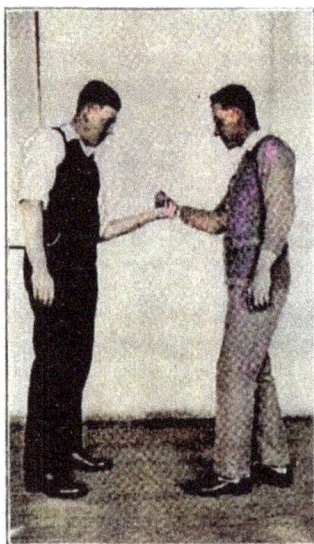

Fig. 2

No. 1.—WRIST HOLD.

(b) Your assailant seizes you by both wrists (Fig. 3).
To make him release his hold:—Bend your arms towards
your body and twist your wrists in the direction of his
thumbs. Or:—Jerk your hands towards your body, at the
same time hitting him in the face with the top of your head
(Fig. 4).

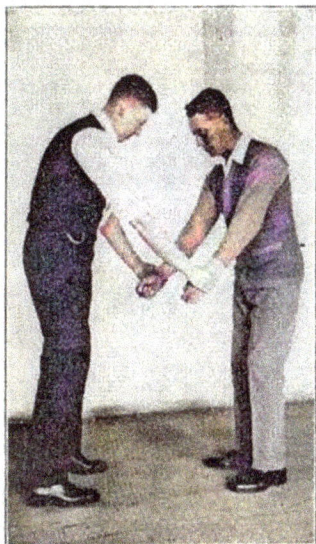

Fig. 4

Fig. 3

No. 2.—Being Strangled.

(*a*) Your assailant seizes you by the throat with his right hand, forcing you back against a wall (Fig. 5).

1. With a sweeping blow of your right hand strike his right wrist towards your left-hand side.
2. If necessary, knee him in the testicles with your right knee (Fig. 6.)

Fig. 6

Fig. 5

No. 2.—Being Strangled.

(b) Your assailant seizes you by the throat with both hands, forcing you back against a wall.

1. Bring your forearms up inside his arms and strike outwards.
2. If necessary, knee him in the testicles with your right knee (Fig. 7).

Fig. 7

No. 3.—"Bear Hug." From in Front.

Your assailant seizes you around the body and arms with both arms (Fig. 8).

1. Knee him in the testicles or stomach.
2. Kick him on the shins.
3. Stamp on his feet.
4. Bump him in the face with your head.
5. Seize him by the testicles with your right or left hand.

Fig. 8

6

No. 4.—"BEAR HUG." FROM BEHIND.

Your assailant seizes you around the body with both arms (Fig. 9).

1. Kick him on the shins.
2. Stamp on his feet.
3. Bump him in the face with the back of your head.
4. Seize him by the testicles with your right or left hand.

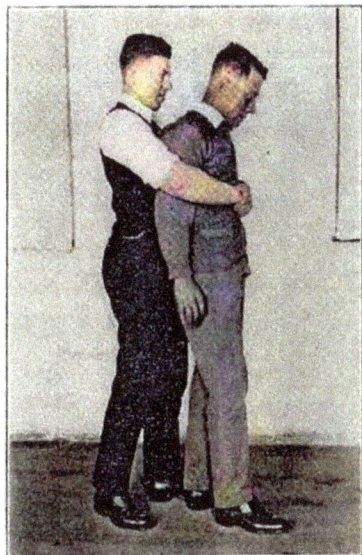

FIG. 9

No. 5.—WAIST HOLD. FROM IN FRONT.

Your assailant seizes you around the body from in front, leaving your arms free.

1. Strike his chin a hard upward jab with the heel of your right wrist (Fig. 10).
2. Seize his neck with both hands, fingers touching behind, thumbs in the front, one on each side of the "Adam's Apple." Force inwards with the point of your thumb and jerk his head sharply backwards (Fig. 11).
3. Seize the back of his neck between the thumb and the fingers of your right hand and force him to the ground (Fig. 12).
4. Kick him on the shins.
5. Knee him in the testicles or stomach.

No. 5.—WAIST HOLD. FROM IN FRONT.

FIG. 10

FIG. 11

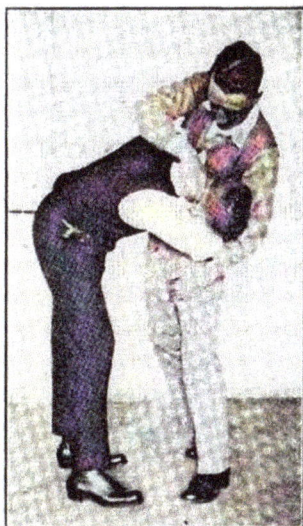

FIG. 12

No. 6.—WAIST HOLD. FROM BEHIND.

Your assailant seizes you around the waist from behind, leaving your arms free.

1. Strike the back of his hand with your knuckles (Fig. 13).
2. Seize either of his little fingers and bend it backwards; if necessary, break it (Fig. 14).
3. Stamp on his feet with the heel of your boot.
4. If your assailant has sufficiently long hair for you to get a good hold of it, reach over backwards with your left hand and seize it, bend suddenly forwards, pulling him by the hair over your back (Fig. 15).

No. 6.—Waist Hold. From Behind.

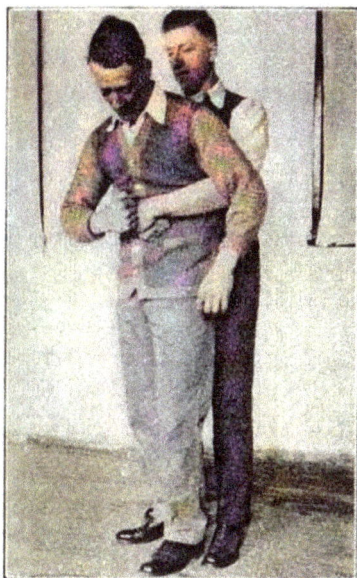

FIG. 13

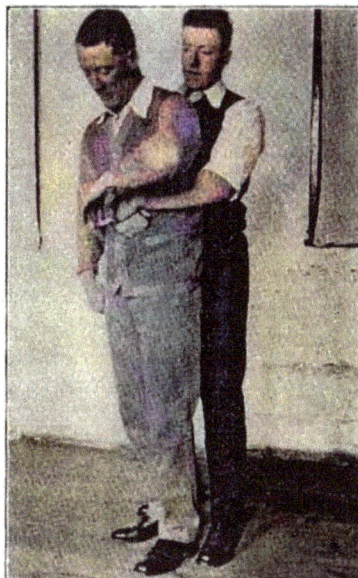

FIG. 14

FIG. 15

No. 7.—HAIR HOLD. FROM BEHIND.

Your assailant seizes you by the hair, from behind, with his right hand.

1. Seize his hand with both of yours to prevent him letting go (Fig. 16).
2. Turn in towards your assailant; this will twist his wrist.
3. Force your head up and bend his wrist inwards, away from his elbow (Fig. 17).

No. 7.—Hair Hold. From Behind.

Fig. 16

Fig. 17

No. 8.—COAT HOLD.

Your assailant seizes you by the left shoulder with his right hand.

1. Seize his right hand with your right hand.
2. Seize his right elbow with your left hand, thumb to the right (Fig. 18).
3. With a circular upward and downward motion of your left hand on the elbow, turn sharply outwards towards your right-hand side (Fig. 19).
4. Keeping a firm grip with your right hand, which will prevent him from releasing his hold, force down on his elbow with your left hand.

Note.—An "Edge of the Hand Blow" given as shown in Figure 20 will be found to be very effective.

No. 8.—COAT HOLD.

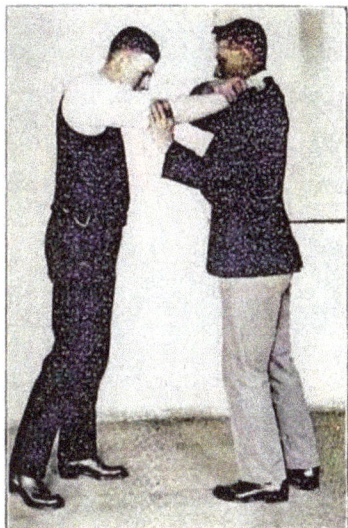

FIG. 18

FIG. 19

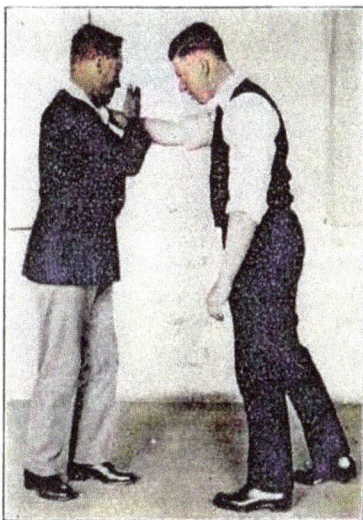

FIG. 20

No. 9—Coat Hold.

Your assailant seizes you by the left shoulder with his right hand.

1. Seize his right elbow with your left hand from underneath; at the same time pass your right hand over the arm and seize the elbow with your right hand above your left (Fig. 21).
2. With a circular upward and downward motion of your hands on his elbow turn sharply outwards towards your right-hand side. This will bring you into the position shown in Fig. 22.
3. Force his elbow towards your body and push up with your left shoulder. This will prevent him from releasing his arm. If necessary, knee him in the face with your right knee.

No. 9.—Coat Hold.

Fig. 21

Fig. 22

17

No. 10.—Coat Hold.

Your assailant seizes you by the lapel of your coat with his right hand.

1. Seize his right wrist with your right hand (Fig. 23).
2. Keeping a firm grip, turn rapidly towards your right-hand side by bringing your right leg to your right rear, simultaneously passing your left arm under his right arm, placing the palm of your left hand on his right thigh (Fig. 24).
3. Force down on the upper part of his right arm with your left shoulder.

Note.—Should your assailant attempt to step forward with his left leg release the hold with your right hand and seize his left ankle and pull it upwards; at the same time push him backwards with your left hand (Fig. 25).

No. 10.—Coat Hold.

Fig. 23

Fig. 24

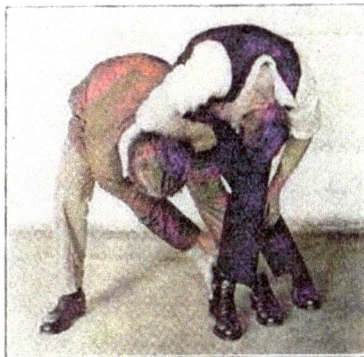

Fig. 25

No. 11.—BELT HOLD.

Your assailant seizes you by the belt with his right hand.

1. Seize his hand with your right hand to prevent him from releasing his hold.
2. Seize his right elbow with your left hand from underneath, thumb to the right (Fig. 26).
3. With a circular upward motion of your left hand force his elbow towards your right side, keeping a firm grip on his hand (Fig. 27).

Note.—Providing you have prevented him from releasing his hold of the belt, this will be found to be a very effective hold.

No. 11.—Belt Hold.

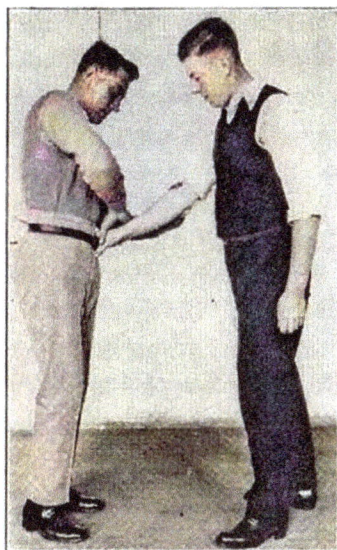

Fig. 26

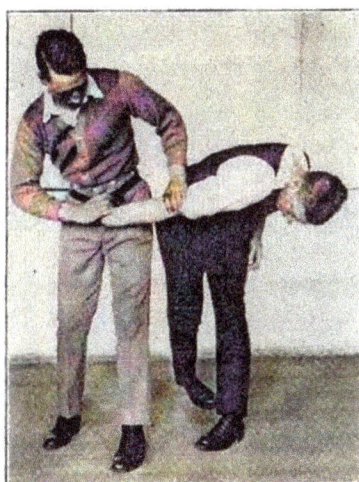

Fig. 27

No. 12.—Neck Hold. From Behind.

Your assailant seizes you around the neck with his right arm from behind (Fig. 28).

1. Lean back on your assailant, seize his right wrist with your left hand and place your right forearm as in (Fig. 29).

2. Suddenly turn about, on your right heel, towards your right-hand side, simultaneously forcing his right wrist with a circular motion upward and downward of your left hand in the same direction as your body. This will force his right arm over your right arm and allow you to seize his wrist with your right hand above your left (Fig. 30).

3. Force the upper part of his right arm against your body and his elbow into your chest and jerk his wrist towards the ground.

No. 12.—Neck Hold. From Behind.

FIG. 28

FIG. 29

FIG. 30

No. 13.—SIMPLE COUNTERS.

1. It frequently happens that you meet a person who is very proud of his gripping powers and takes great pleasure when shaking hands in gripping your hand with all his strength and causing you to wince.

    To prevent this:—Force your right thumb into the back of his hand as in Fig. 31.

2. When walking you see two persons approaching you who intend to jostle you between them.

    To prevent this:—Place your hands on their shoulders, your forearms under their chins as in Fig. 32, and suddenly shoot your forearms outwards.

3. A person attempts to lift you up by catching hold of you under the armpits.

    To prevent this:—Force the points of your thumbs up into his neck, close alongside the jawbone, as in Fig. 33.

No. 13.—Simple Counters.

Fig. 31

Fig. 32

Fig. 33

METHOD OF DEALING WITH AN ARMED
ASSAILANT

The "Defendu" method of dealing with an armed assailant may at first glance appear to be risky, but one will be surprised to discover how safe and simple this method is when put into practice by a person who has studied it and who has to cope with a man unacquainted with it.

The author, being aware that anything original is generally doubted, made it a point, when giving a demonstration, to have his assailant armed with a loaded air pistol, and at no time, even when the pistol was fired, did the pellet ever strike his body; in fact, in the majority of cases the opponent was disarmed before he could possibly fire.

It should always be borne in mind that a man who "holds" you "up" with a pistol or other weapon is, to use a slang term, "throwing a bluff" and is far too cowardly to commit murder; otherwise he would shoot on sight and rob you afterwards. He is aware that if a shot is fired it is liable to alarm the neighborhood, which is what he wants to prevent at all costs. Further, he is aware that a person carrying valuables might be armed, and for this reason he will be sure to make you hold your hands above your head so as to prevent you from drawing. Finally, in order to search you he must come within reach of your hands. The unexpectedness of finding that he is attacked by an apparently defenceless person will come as such a surprise to him that it will be the simplest thing possible to disarm him before he is aware what has happened.

The following is an extract from the *Over-Seas Daily Mail*, February 2, 1924.

GIRL BANDIT'S COUPS

"HOLD YOUR HANDS UP NICELY"

The girl bandit with bobbed hair and a sealskin coat who within the last three weeks has robbed over a dozen New York shops reappeared at a provision merchant's establishment in Albany Avenue, Brooklyn.

She asked for a cake of soap. When the assistant handed her the article he found himself facing a pistol, while the sweet-voiced girl remarked, "Hold your hands up nicely; be a good boy, and go into the back room."

He did so, and the girl's customary male companion took $35 from his pocket and $55 from the till.

$20,000 JEWEL HAUL

Later the blonde girl undertook an excursion to Philadelphia in pursuit of a New York jeweler, Mr. Abraham Kaplan, who was carrying with him a suitcase containing $20,000 worth of jewels.

She accosted him as he was leaving Broad Street Station at Philadelphia and asked him the way to the post office. He told her he was unable to direct her, and, according to his story, she then drew a pistol from her handbag and ordered him to turn about. With the muzzle of her pistol pressed against his back, she forced him to walk into a narrow passage, where two men relieved him of his suitcase, a diamond scarf-pin, a watch, and $100 in cash.

"Holdups" of this description are of frequent occurrence in various parts of the world, and it is owing to this fact that the author is publishing the "Defendu" method of self-defence. Now, had this New York jeweler been acquainted with only a part of the "Defendu" method, it would have been a simple matter for him to have disarmed this girl bandit immediately she pressed the pistol against his back, and, what is of more importance, he would not, in doing so, have increased the risk that he ran of being shot.

27

No. 1.—Disarming a Person Found Pointing a Pistol
at Another.

Should you find a man pointing with a pistol at another,
and unaware of your presence:—

1. Seize his hand and pistol with your right hand from
   underneath, at the same time seizing his right elbow
   with your left hand (Fig. 34).

2. Jerk his hand upwards and backwards and force his
   elbow upwards with your left hand, simultaneously
   pivoting inwards on your left foot. This will break
   his trigger finger and cause him to release his hold on
   the weapon.

3. If necessary, knee him in the testicles with your right
   knee (Fig. 35).

No. 1.—DISARMING A PERSON FOUND POINTING A PISTOL
AT ANOTHER.

FIG. 34

FIG. 35

No. 2.—DISARMING AN ASSAILANT HOLDING YOU UP WITH
   A PISTOL.   FROM IN FRONT.

Your assailant gives the order, "Hands Up," and covers
you by pointing a pistol at your stomach:

1. Hold up your hands above your head, keeping them
   as far apart as possible (Fig. 36).

2. Lead your assailant to suppose that you are scared
   to death.

3. With a swinging blow seize the pistol and hand with
   your right hand, simultaneously turning rapidly sideways towards your left-hand side.   This will knock
   the pistol outwards past your body (Fig. 37).

4. Seize the pistol and hand from underneath with your
   left hand, knee him in the testicles, and letting go with
   your right hand seize his right elbow.   Force his hand
   and pistol upwards and backwards with your left
   hand, and pull his elbow towards you (Fig. 38).   If
   necessary, knee him in the testicles with your right
   knee.

Note.—The reason for keeping your hands held up as far apart
   as possible is that your assailant cannot look at two objects
   at one time.   If he is watching your left hand, use your right;
   if the right, use the left; should he be looking at your body or
   face, use either.   Should it be too dark for you to see which
   hand he is looking at, use which you think best; he will not be
   expecting any attack.

No. 2.—Disarming an Assailant Holding You up with a Pistol. From in Front.

Fig. 36

Fig. 37

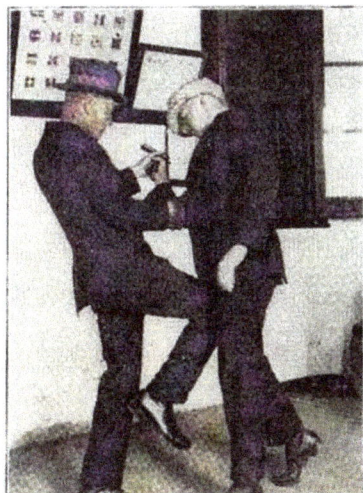

Fig. 38

No. 3.—Disarming an Assailant Holding You up with
a Pistol.   From in Front.

Having been "held up" as in Fig. 39, and while your
assailant is watching your right hand, the following method
should be applied:—

1. With a swinging blow seize your assailant's right
   wrist with your left hand, simultaneously turning
   rapidly sideways towards your right-hand side.   This
   will knock the pistol inwards past your body (Fig.
   40).

2. Seize the pistol and hand from underneath with your
   right hand, and with a circular backward and downward motion break his trigger finger and knee him in
   the testicles (Fig. 41).

No. 3.—Disarming an Assailant Holding You up with a Pistol. From in Front.

Fig. 39

Fig. 40

Fig. 41

No. 4.—Disarming an Assailant Holding You up with a Pistol. From Behind.

Your assailant gives the order "Hands up" and covers you by holding a pistol in the small of your back:

1. Hold up your hands above your head and exhibit the utmost terror (Fig. 42).
2. Turning rapidly inwards towards your left-hand side, passing your left arm over and around your assailant's right forearm, holding it with a firm grip of your left arm against the left side of your body, simultaneously knee him in the testicles with your right knee and "chin jab" him with your right hand (Fig. 43).

Note.—If you keep a fairly firm grip with your left arm on your assailant's right arm it will be impossible for him to shoot you or release his arm, and, as previously stated, the shock from the blow on the testicles or even the "chin jab" will cause him to immediately release his hold on the pistol.

No. 4.—DISARMING AN ASSAILANT HOLDING YOU UP WITH
A PISTOL. FROM BEHIND.

FIG. 42

FIG. 43

No. 5.—Disarming an Assailant Holding You up with a Pistol. From Behind.

Having been "held up" as in Fig. 44, and for some reason or other not finding it convenient to turn towards your left-hand side, the following method should be applied:

1. Turning rapidly outwards towards your right-hand side, lower your right hand and pass it under your assailant's right forearm and seize his arm above the elbow, lifting up his forearm with your right arm (Fig. 45).

2. Simultaneously seize the pistol underneath with your left hand and bend his wrist backwards. If necessary, knee him in the testicles (Fig. 46).

No. 5.—DISARMING AN ASSAILANT HOLDING YOU UP WITH A PISTOL. FROM BEHIND.

FIG. 44

FIG. 45

FIG. 46

No. 6.—Arresting a Man Known to Carry Firearms.

Your opponent is coming towards you and you are aware that he will, if possible, shoot to avoid arrest.

When about 10 to 12 feet away from him give him the order to halt and "Hands Up," covering him with your weapon. Tell him to turn about and march in front of you with his hands held above his head; and whilst he is being searched, keep him covered from behind.

Note.—In no circumstances permit him to get within less than 10 feet of you previous to his having been handcuffed. Even if halted at a distance of 12 feet, a determined criminal may possibly endeavor to close on you by means of a "rolling dive" (Figs. 47, 48, 49, 50 and 51). Should this be attempted, a rapid leap to one side will get you into a position similar to your original one and well placed for delivering an effective shot.

Caution.—This fall must first be learnt as shown on page 141.

38

No. 6.—ARRESTING A MAN KNOWN TO CARRY FIREARMS.

FIG. 47

FIG. 48

FIG. 49

FIG. 50

FIG. 51

No. 7.—DISARMING A MAN ATTACKING YOU WITH A KNIFE. "STAGE STYLE."

Your assailant rushes at you with a knife in his right hand:

1. Seize his right wrist with your left hand, bend his arm at the elbow towards him (Fig. 52).
2. Pass your right arm under the upper part of his right arm, seize his right wrist with your right hand above your left.
3. Force the upper part of his right arm against your body, and his elbow into your chest so that it will be at a right angle with your body.
4. Jerk his wrist towards the ground, and knee him in the testicles with your right knee (Fig. 53).

Note.—The above method will be found very effective should you ever be so fortunate as to be attacked in the above manner, but unfortunately, except on the stage, persons who carry a knife for the purpose of attack do not hold it as in Fig. 52.

It should be noted that the knife is held as in Fig. 54, edge of the blade uppermost. The part of the body usually aimed at is the pit of the stomach, with the intention of ripping it up. If attacked in this manner, and you are unarmed, there are only two methods of defense:—1st, RUN; or 2nd, with a lightning-like movement of either foot, kick your assailant in the testicles or stomach as in Fig. 55.

No. 7.—Disarming a Man Attacking You with a Knife.

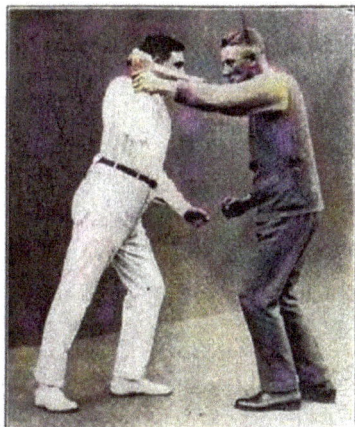

Fig. 52

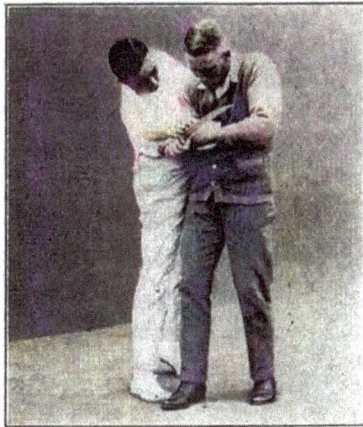

Fig. 53

Fig. 54

Fig. 55

No. 1.—POLICE HOLD. ("COME ALONG" GRIP.)

1. Stand facing your opponent.
2. Seize his right wrist with your right hand (Fig. 56).
3. Step in towards him with your left foot.
4. Pass your left arm over his right arm (above the elbow joint), catching hold of your right arm by the biceps with your left hand.
5. Keep your opponent's right arm straight and the knuckles downwards.
6. Stand upright and force your left forearm bone into the back muscles of his right arm by lifting upwards with your left arm and pressing downwards with right hand, towards your opponent's body, on his right wrist.
7. Apply the pressure until your opponent is standing on his toes (Fig. 57).

Note.—Should you, owing to the shortness of your forearm or for any other reason, find it difficult to catch hold of your biceps with your left hand (Fig. 57), seize the left lapel of your jacket instead. Never lean towards your opponent; by so doing you place yourself in a very cramped position. If your opponent attempts to throw himself forward or backwards, apply pressure with a jerk. This will strain the elbow joint and render his right arm useless for attack.

No. 1.—Police Hold.   ("Come Along" Grip.)

Fig. 56 '

Fig. 57

43

No. 2.—POLICE HOLD WITH TRIP.

Having secured the Police Hold (Fig. 57):

1. Shoot your left leg across your opponent's legs, back of your leg to the front of his, your left foot flat on the ground and leg braced stiff (Fig. 58).

2. Bend forward and outwards from the waist, letting go with your left arm and pulling your opponent sharply towards your right-hand side by his right arm (Fig. 59).

Note.—The importance of keeping the leg braced stiff and the foot flat on the ground can be clearly seen from the following illustrations:

Fig. 60.—Leg and Foot, *Correct Position*—Leg capable of taking a strain of 300 to 400 pounds.

Fig. 61.—Leg and Foot, *Not Correct*—The leg in this position will not stand more than about a 30-pound strain.

No. 2.—Police Hold with Trip.

Fig. 58

Fig. 59

Fig. 60

Fig. 61

No. 3.—POLICE HOLD WITH FALL.

Having secured the Police Hold (Fig. 62), and having been tripped owing to your failure to keep sufficient pressure on his arm:—

1. Retain your hold with both hands.
2. Turn your head, keeping your chin down towards your left shoulder (Fig. 63), and let yourself fall— you cannot hurt yourself. Fig. 64 shows the position you would be in after the fall.

Note.—In practice care must be taken not to throw yourself forward when your opponent trips you, otherwise he is liable to be rendered unconscious by striking his head on the ground.

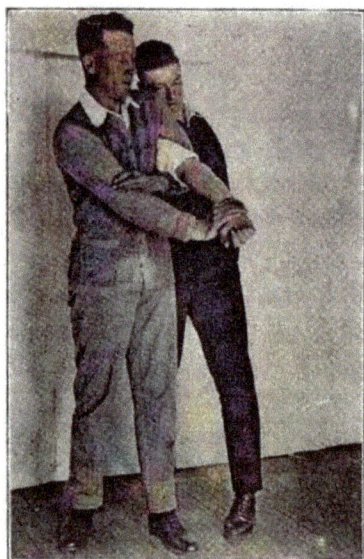

FIG. 62

No. 3.—Police Hold with Fall.

Fig. 63

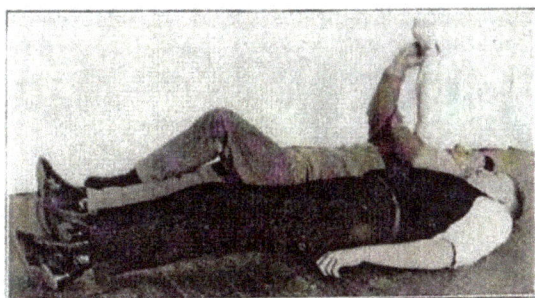

Fig. 64

No. 4.—HANDCUFF HOLD.

1. Stand facing your opponent.
2. Seize his right wrist with both of your hands—right hand above left (Fig. 65).
3. Swing his arm up high.
4. Pass under it by turning inwards with your back towards him (Fig. 66).
5. Step to his back with your left foot, and with a circular upward motion force his wrist well up his back.
6. Retain grasp on his wrist with your left hand and seize his right elbow with your right hand.
7. Bend his wrist towards his right shoulder and lift upwards with your right hand on his elbow.
8. Apply the pressure until your opponent is in the position shown in Fig. 67.

Note.—To throw your opponent:—Apply pressure with your left hand on his right (forward and towards the ground), at the same time lifting up his elbow.

All the above movements are one continuous swing of your opponent's right arm, and although from the positions shown in Figs. 65, 66 and 67, it may appear to the novice that your opponent could easily hit you with his disengaged hand or kick you with his feet, it will be found that it is almost impossible for him to do either. Should he, however, attempt to do so, and the circumstances justify it, "counter" as follows:—

While in the position shown in Fig. 65, release your hold with your left hand, pulling him towards you with your right hand, pass your left arm over his right arm and secure the Police Hold (Fig. 57), and apply pressure with a jerk.

While in the position shown in Fig. 66, shoot your left leg in front of his legs, simultaneously throwing yourself forward to the ground to your right front. This will throw him, with a smashing blow, on to his face, and, providing you have not allowed his wrist to turn in your hands, will probably dislocate his shoulders.

While in the position shown in Fig. 67, apply pressure on his wrist and elbow with a jerk and throw yourself forward to the ground. This will throw him on to his face and probably dislocate his wrist or shoulder.

48

No. 4.—Handcuff Hold.

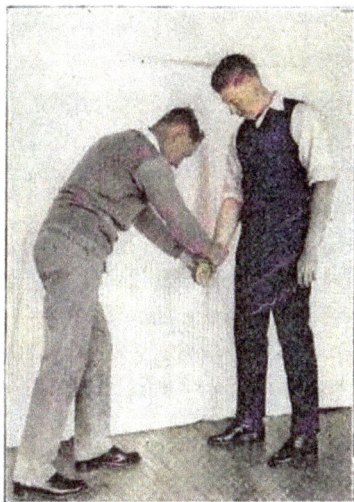

FIG. 65

FIG. 66

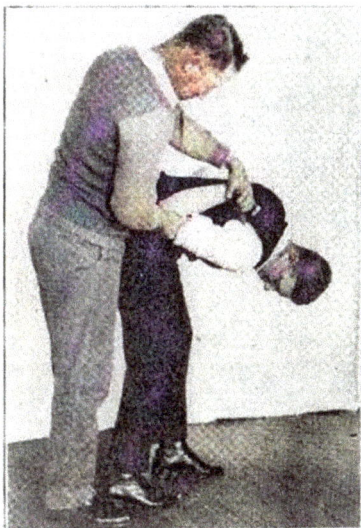

FIG. 67

No. 5.—HANDCUFF HOLD (FOR A SMALLER OPPONENT).

If your opponent is too small for you to pass under his arm, as in Fig. 68, apply the following hold:

1. Stand facing your opponent, slightly to his right-hand side.
2. Seize his right wrist with your left hand, your knuckles downwards and thumb to the left.
3. Seize his right elbow with your right hand, your knuckles towards your left-hand side (Fig. 69).
4. Force his hand up his back by pulling his elbow towards you and jerking his hand upwards. This will pull your opponent into the position shown in Fig. 70.

FIG. 68

No. 5.—Handcuff Hold (For a Smaller Opponent).

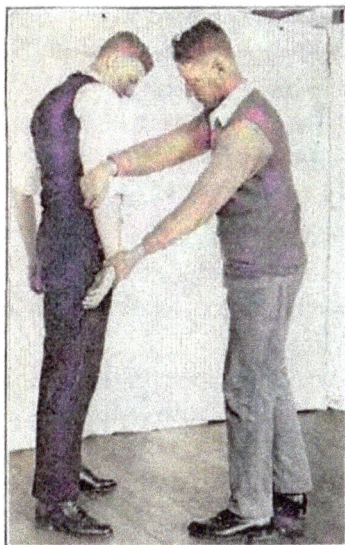

FIG. 69

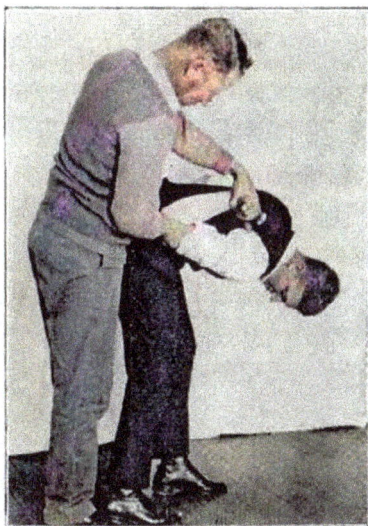

FIG. 70

No. 6.—Handcuff Hold (Handcuffing a Prisoner).

The reason for this hold being named the Handcuff Hold is that this is the only way one man can handcuff another, unless the latter is willing to submit.

When handcuffing a prisoner it should be done so that his hands are locked behind his back. This will handicap him in running should he attempt to get away.

To handcuff your opponent:

1. Secure the hold as in Fig. 70.
2. Throw your opponent, retaining the hold on his wrist and elbow.
3. Sit astride your opponent's back (Fig. 71), holding his elbow in position with your right thigh. This will allow you to release your hold with your right hand and snap the handcuff on his right wrist (Fig. 72.)
4. Reach over and seize his left wrist with your left hand and jerk it across his back and snap on the other handcuff.

Note.—Should you have any difficulty in securing your opponent's wrist, seize his chin from underneath with your right hand and the side of his head with your left hand. Jerk upwards with your right hand and push his head downwards with your left hand (Fig. 73).

An alternative method (if your opponent's hair is long enough for you to grip it) is to seize his hair as far forward as possible with your right hand, placing the left hand on the back of his neck and jerking upwards with your right hand and forcing downwards with your left (Fig. 74).

After a very little of either of the above methods your opponent will be quite willing to submit to being handcuffed.

Care should be taken not to break a person's neck by the above method.

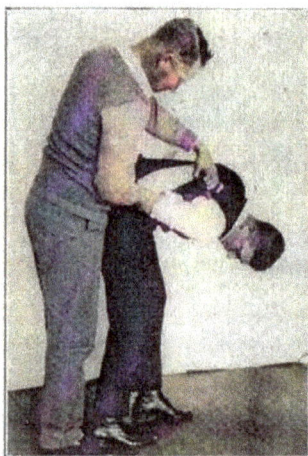

Fig. 70

52

No. 6.—Handcuff Hold (Handcuffing a Prisoner).

FIG. 71

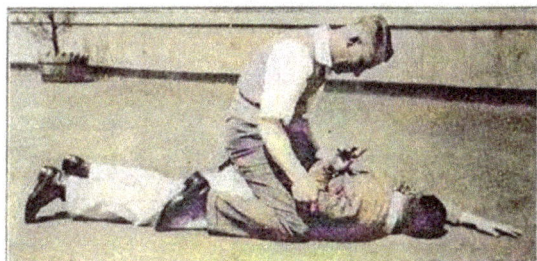

FIG. 72

FIG. 73

FIG. 74

No. 7.—ARM HOLD.

1. Stand level with your opponent on his right side and facing the same way.

2. Seize his right wrist with your right hand, back of your hand to the front, back of his hand downwards.

3. Raise his right arm with your right hand and at the same time pass your left arm under his right and place your left hand behind his neck (Fig. 75).

4. Straighten your left arm and pull downwards on his right arm with your right hand (Fig. 76).

Note.—Your left arm must be above your opponent's right elbow; otherwise you cannot obtain any leverage.

No. 7.—Arm Hold.

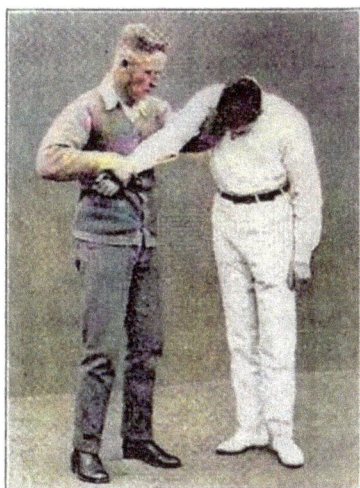

Fig. 75

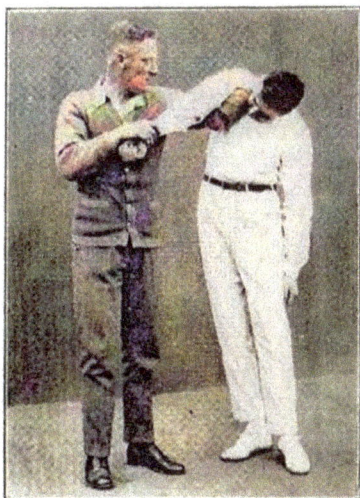

Fig. 76

No. 8.—Bent Arm Hold.

You are facing your opponent and he raises his right hand as if about to deliver a blow.

1. Seize his right wrist with your left hand, bending his arm at the elbow, towards him (Fig. 77).
2. Pass your right arm under the upper part of his right arm, seizing his right wrist with your right hand above your left.
3. Force the upper part of his right arm against your body, and his elbow into your chest so that it will be at a right angle with your body.
4. Jerk his wrist towards the ground (Fig. 78).

No. 8.—Bent Arm Hold.

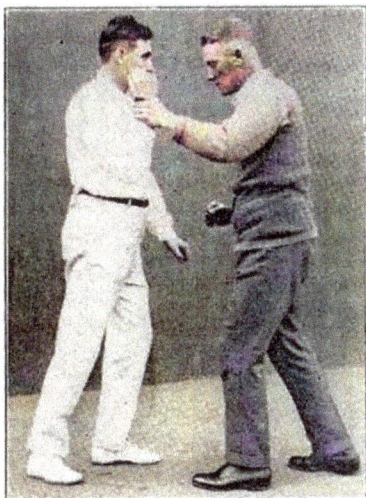

Fig. 77

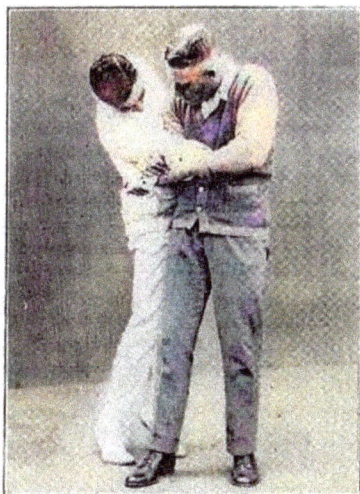

Fig. 78

57

No. 9.—FRONT STRANGLE HOLD.

For defense against a right-handed punch to the head, or a downward swinging blow at the head with a stick, etc.

1. Duck your head to the left and rush in under your assailant's right arm to his right side (Fig. 79).

2. Pass your right arm around his neck, catching your right wrist with your left hand.

3. Apply pressure by pulling on your right wrist with your left hand, forcing his right arm up alongside his neck with your shoulder and head (Fig. 80).

Note.—Keep the fingers and thumb of your right hand rigid and force your right forearm bone into the muscle of his neck.

Bring your right hip into the small of his back and bend him backwards (Fig. 80).

No. 9.—FRONT STRANGLE HOLD.

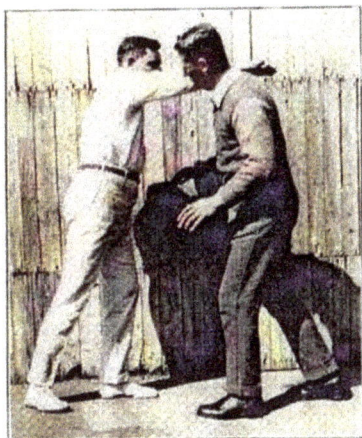

FIG. 79

FIG. 80

No. 10.—Front Strangle Hold with Throw.

Having secured the hold as in Fig. 81, and you want to throw your assailant:

1. Retain the hold with your right arm around his neck and place your left hand at the back of his right thigh (Fig. 82).
2. Lift upwards with your left hand, pulling downwards with your right arm, at the same time shooting your hip into the small of his back by straightening out your legs.
3. When your assailant is off his feet, bend forward from the waist and throw him over your shoulder (Fig. 83).

Note.—It is quite a simple matter for you to throw an assailant in the above manner, even if he should be twice your own weight, but care must be taken when practicing it to keep a firm grip with your right arm to prevent him from falling on his head.

Having decided to give your assailant a rather heavy fall, release your hold when in the position shown in Figure 83; this will throw him on his stomach, with his head towards you. Should your assailant be one of several who have made an unwarranted attack on you, release your hold with your right arm at the moment when he is in the position shown in Figure 84, and dislocate his neck.

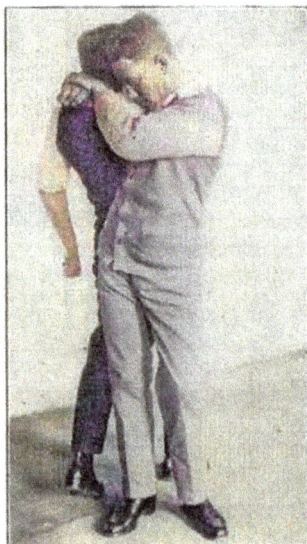

Fig. 81

60

HOLDS THAT ARE EFFECTIVE

No. 10.—Front Strangle Hold with Throw.

Fig. 82

Fig. 83

Fig. 84

61

No. 11.—FRONT STRANGLE HOLD ON THE GROUND.

Having secured the hold as in Fig. 85, and you are tripped, or want to bring your assailant to the ground.

1. Retain the hold on your assailant's neck and arm, shoot both of your legs forward, letting your assailant take the force of the fall on his back.

2. Force your head down on to your assailant's right arm and head; at the same time force the weight of your body on to his chest, applying pressure by pulling up on your right wrist with your left hand (Fig. 86).

Note.—Should the circumstances justify, and it is necessary that you should release your hold, apply pressure sharply with your right arm on your assailant's neck until he faints (10 to 15 seconds).

It should be noted that your assailant while in this position (Fig. 86), cannot do you any injury whatever and providing you keep your left foot flat on the ground and your legs out of reach of his legs he cannot get up.

No. 11.—FRONT STRANGLE HOLD ON THE GROUND.

FIG. 85

FIG. 86

63

No. 12.—BACK STRANGLE HOLD.

1. Stand at your opponent's back.
2. Place your left arm around his neck, with your forearm bone bearing on his Adam's apple.
3. Place the back of your right arm (above the elbow) on his right shoulder and clasp your right biceps with your left hand.
4. Grasp the back of his head with your right hand.
5. Pull up with your left forearm and press forward on the back of his head with your right hand (Fig. 87).

Note.—If this hold is applied correctly it is impossible for your opponent to release himself; further, his neck can easily be dislocated and if pressure is applied for 10 seconds he will int owing to anæmia of the brain.

It should be noted that this is a drastic hold and would only be used against an opponent who would go to any extent to gain his freedom. Should.he attempt to seize you by the testicles, step back quickly, at the same time jolting his head forward with your right hand and dislocate his neck (Fig. 88).

No. 12.—Back Strangle Hold.

Fig. 87

Fig. 88

No. 13.—Back Strangle Hold Applied from the Front.

1. Stand facing your opponent. Seize his right shoulder with your left hand and his left shoulder with your right hand (Fig. 89).
2. Push with your left hand (retaining the hold) and pull towards you with your right hand. If this is done suddenly your opponent will be turned completely around and your left arm will be in position around his neck.
3. Place the back of your right arm (above the elbow) on his right shoulder and clasp your right biceps with your left hand.
4. Grasp the back of his head with your right hand.
5. Pull up with your left forearm and press forward on the back of his head with your right hand (Fig. 90).

No. 13.—BACK STRANGLE HOLD APPLIED FROM THE FRONT.

FIG. 89

FIG. 90

No. 14.—WRIST AND ELBOW HOLD.

Your assailant seizes you by the throat with his right hand.

1. Seize assailant's right hand from above with your right hand, your fingers passing over the back of his hand to the palm.

2. Seize his right elbow with your left hand, thumb to the right (Fig. 91).

3. With a circular upward swing of your right hand towards your right-hand side, simultaneously turn inwards and press with your left hand on his elbow, bending his right wrist towards him (Figs. 92 and 92A).

4. To throw your assailant, jerk his right arm to the ground by falling forward on to your knees.

No. 14.—Wrist and Elbow Hold.

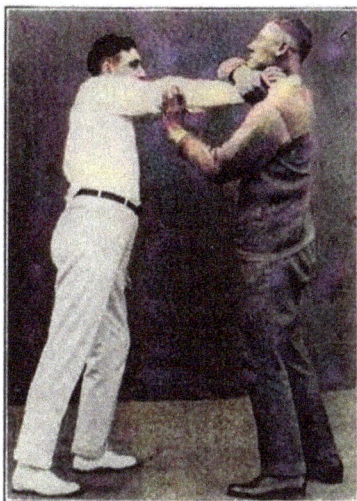

Fig 91

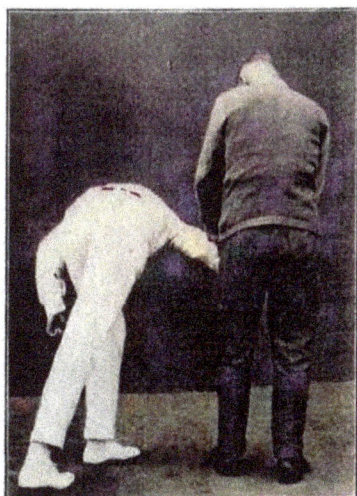

Fig. 92

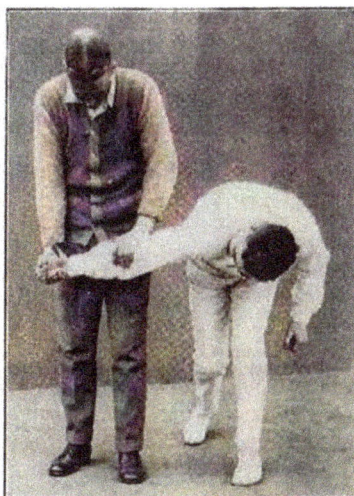

Fig. 92a

No. 15.—Wrist and Elbow Hold, Whilst Lying in Bed.

Your assailant seizes you by the throat with his right hand whilst you are lying in bed.

1. Seize his right hand from above, with your right hand, your fingers passing over the back of his hand to the palm.

2. Seize his right elbow with your left hand, thumb to the right (Figs. 93 and 93a).

3. Turn sharply to your right on to your stomach, pulling his right arm under your body, by pulling on the wrist and forcing towards your right-hand side with your left hand on his elbow. This will bring you and your assailant into the positions shown in Fig. 94.

4. Keeping his right arm straight, force down on his elbow with your left hand and twist his right wrist towards him by an upward motion of your right hand.

No. 15.—Wrist and Elbow Hold, Whilst Lying in Bed.

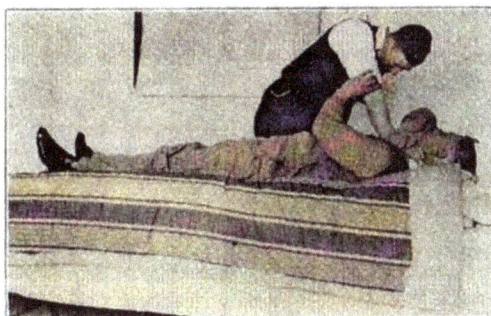

Fig. 93

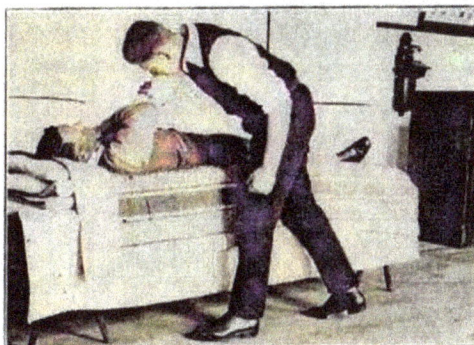

Fig. 93a

Fig. 94

No. 16.—THUMB AND ELBOW HOLD.

Stand facing your opponent and slightly to his left.

1. Insert your right thumb between the thumb and forefinger of his left hand, palm of your right hand upwards, thumb to the right (Fig. 95).

2. Seize his left elbow with your left hand, knuckles to the right (Fig. 96).

3. Step in towards your opponent; at the same time turn your body so that you are facing in the same direction, simultaneously forcing his left forearm up across his chest and towards his left shoulder by pulling his elbow with your left hand over your right forearm and forcing upwards with your right hand.

4. Keeping a firm grip on the upper part of his left arm with your right arm, apply a slight pressure on the back of his hand towards your left-hand side with your right hand and you will be surprised to see how quickly your opponent will raise on his toes and shout for mercy (Fig. 97).

5. Should your opponent be a very powerful man and try to resist, a little extra pressure (3 to 4 lbs.) applied with the left hand on his elbow, as in Fig. 98, will be sufficient to convince him he has met his master, and he will be quite willing to submit to anything.

Note.—This is the most effective hold known, and I think I am correct in saying that only Japanese jui-jitsu experts (4th and 5th degree black belt) know how to apply it. Further, it should be noted that while all the other holds are very effective, and that it is not necessary to exert a great amount of strength to overcome your opponent, the fact remains that should it be necessary for you to have to take an opponent a distance of a mile or so, the strain, both mental and physical, would be so great that it would be very difficult for the average person to accomplish it, but if you have secured the hold as in Fig. 97, you would have no difficulty whatsoever in taking a very powerful opponent, even if he was resisting, as far as it is possible for you to walk.

No. 16.—Thumb and Elbow Hold.

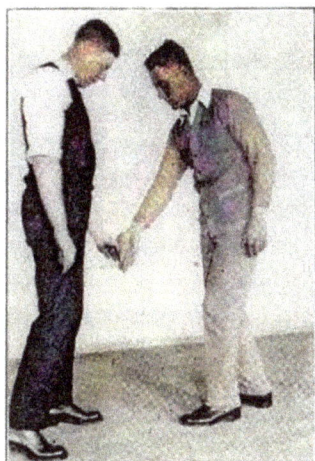

Fig. 95

Fig. 96

Fig. 97

Fig. 98

No. 17.—HEAD HOLD.

Stand facing your opponent.

1. Strike your opponent on the left side of his neck with the inside of your right forearm (Fig. 99).

2. Pass your arm around his head, catching hold of your right wrist with your left hand and forcing his head down to your right (Fig. 100).

3. Force your right forearm bone into the right side of his face by pulling on your right wrist with your left hand and forcing downwards on the left side of his face with your body.

Note.—This hold is very painful for your opponent, and care must be taken in practice to apply the pressure gradually.

No. 17.—HEAD HOLD.

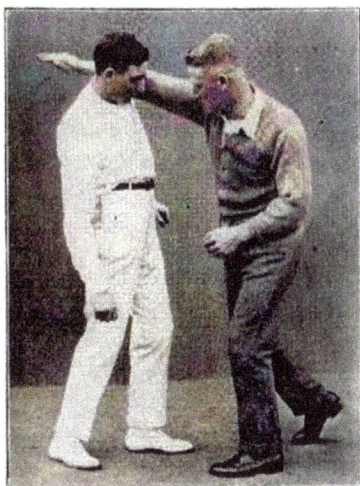

FIG. 99

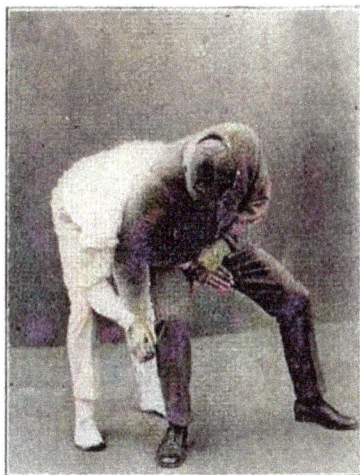

FIG. 100

No. 18.—HEAD HOLD WITH THROW.

Having secured the hold as in Fig. 101, and you are about to be attacked by another opponent:

1. Retain the hold of your first opponent and turn sharply towards your left-hand side, straighten up your body and swing him by the neck off his feet (Fig. 102).

2. Keep turning until your opponent's feet are well clear of the ground; then suddenly release your hold. Immediately close with your second opponent and treat him likewise.

No. 18.—HEAD HOLD WITH THROW.

FIG. 101

FIG. 102

77

No. 1.—WRIST THROW.

1. Stand facing your opponent and slightly to his right-hand side.

2. Lean forward and seize his right hand with your left, back of your hand towards your right-hand side, your fingers around his thumb towards the palm of his hand, your thumb forced in between the knuckle-joint of his first and second fingers (Fig. 103).

3. Raise his arm, by a circular motion, towards your left-hand side, at the same time seizing the little finger side of his right hand with your right. Turn his palm towards him; then force your thumbs into the back of his hand (Fig. 104).

4. Force his hand towards him. This will throw him on to his right-hand side (Fig. 105).

Note.—While Fig. 104 shows the thumbs forced into the back of the hand, it should be noted that it is not always possible to obtain this position quickly; but providing the palm of your opponent's hand is turned towards him, and pressure is applied with the thumbs on the back of his hand or fingers as in Fig. 106, this will be found to be nearly as effective.

If you have any difficulty in throwing your opponent, give his wrist a sharp turn to your left and pull downwards towards your left-hand side. Another method is to sink suddenly on to one knee and pull downwards towards your left-hand side.

Either of these will cause him to lose his balance and fall.

No. 1.—Wrist Throw.

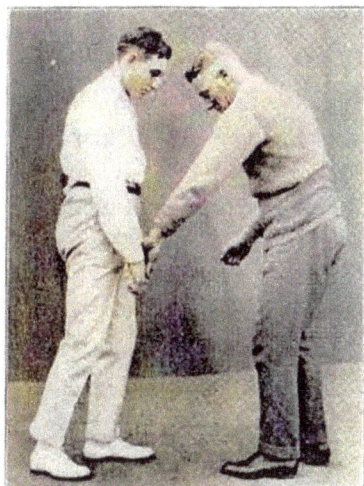

Fig. 103

Fig. 104

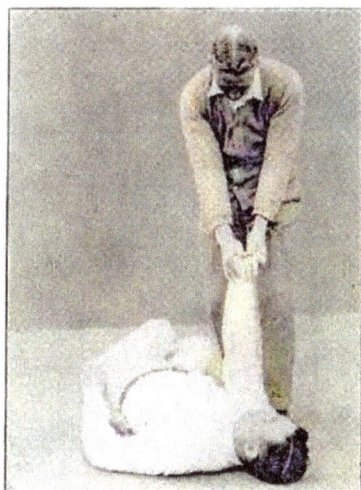

Fig. 105

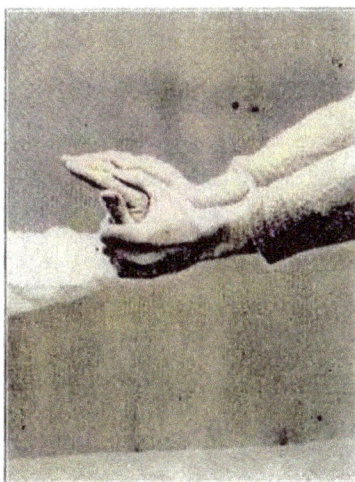

Fig. 106

No. 2.—WRIST THROW WITH LEG HOLD.

Having thrown your opponent as in Fig. 107, and you wish to hold him on the ground:

1. Retain the hold on his right wrist with both hands, step over his body with both feet, keeping his arm between your legs (Fig. 108).
2. Bend your legs from the knees and sit down as close to your opponent's body as possible (Fig. 109).
3. Pull on your opponent's wrist, to keep the arm straight, fall backwards and bend his arm the reverse way by resting the upper part of his arm on your right thigh and forcing his wrist towards the ground (Fig. 110).

Note.—Should your opponent attempt to pull his right arm away by the help of his left hand, force your left or right foot into the bend of his left arm and kick it away (Fig. 111).

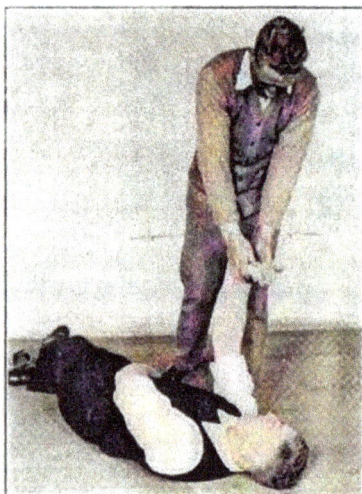

FIG. 107

No. 2.—Wrist Throw with Leg Hold.

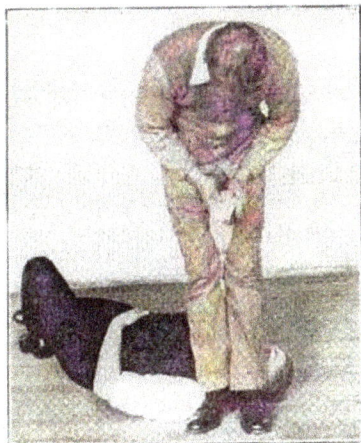

Fig. 108

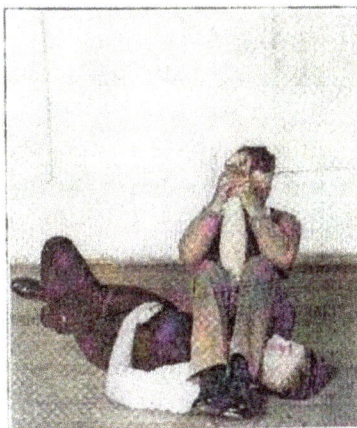

Fig. 109

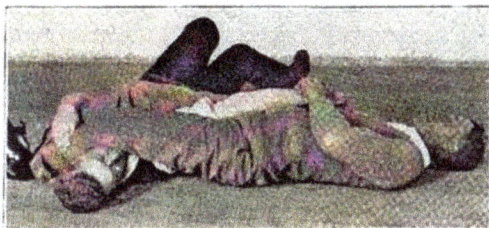

Fig. 110

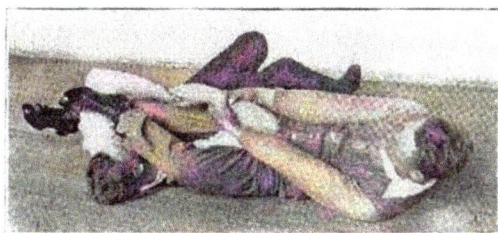

Fig. 111

No. 3.—ARM THROW.

1. Stand facing your opponent and slightly to his right-hand side.
2. Seize his right wrist with both of your hands, right above left (Fig. 112).
3. Swing his arm high up.
4. Pass under it by turning to your right (Fig. 113), keeping a firm hold on his wrist. This will cause his arm to twist as shown in Fig. 114.
5. When in this position sink slightly forward on the left knee, keeping your right leg firm and straight, pull down on your opponent's arm, by bending suddenly towards the ground bending from the waist.
6. This will cause him to fall on his back (Fig. 115).

Note.—This is a very dangerous throw, and great care must be taken when practicing it, otherwise you will dislocate your opponent's shoulder, or cause him to strike the back of his head on the ground.

No. 3.—Arm Throw.

Fig. 112

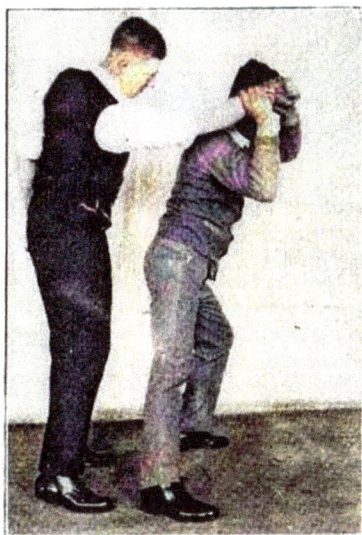

Fig. 113

Fig. 114

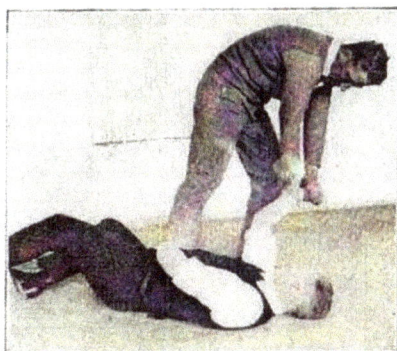

Fig. 115

No. 4.—Hip Throw.

Stand facing your opponent.

1. Seize both his arms above the elbows.
2. Turn your body sharply to your right and shoot your left leg to his left side. Take care that the back of your left leg is against his body and your left foot flat on the ground (Fig. 116).
3. Bend forward towards your right-hand side and jerk him sharply over your left hip, by pulling downwards with your right hand and pushing or lifting upwards with your left hand.
4. This will bring your opponent into the position shown in Fig. 117.

Note.—Having secured the hold as in Fig. 116, and you have difficulty in throwing your opponent, sink suddenly on to your right knee, pulling downwards with your right hand, and pushing or lifting upwards with your left hand (Fig. 118).

Care must be taken when applying this throw in the above manner, otherwise your opponent will be rendered unconscious through striking his head on the ground.

No. 4.—Hip Throw.

Fig. 116

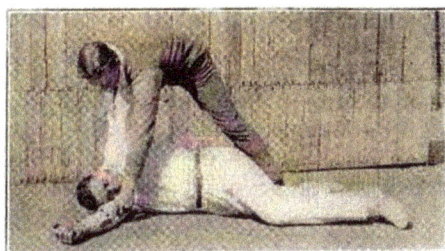

Fig. 117

Fig. 118

No. 5.—HIP THROW, WITH LEG HOLD.

Having secured throw as in Fig. 119:

1. Allow your right hand to slip up his left arm to his wrist and secure it with both hands, right above left. Step over his body with both feet, keeping his arm between your legs (Fig. 120).
2. Bend your legs from the knees and sit down as close to your opponent as possible.
3. Pulling on your opponent's wrist, to keep his left arm straight, fall backwards and bend his arm the reverse way, by resting the upper part of his arm on your left thigh and forcing his wrist towards the ground (Fig. 121).

Note.—Fig. 110 (Wrist Throw with Leg Hold, page 81) and Fig. 121 show that when the leg hold is applied your opponent's arm should be across the thigh which is nearest his body. By so doing you have a much better leverage and it becomes extremely difficult for him to pull his arm away.

No. 5.—Hip Throw, with Leg Hold.

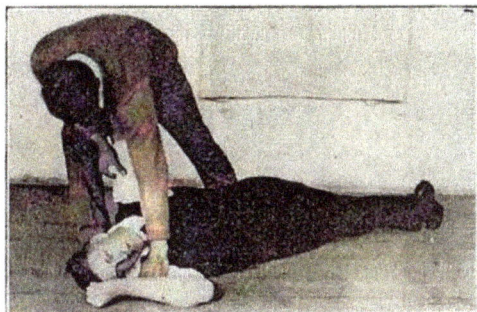

Fig. 119

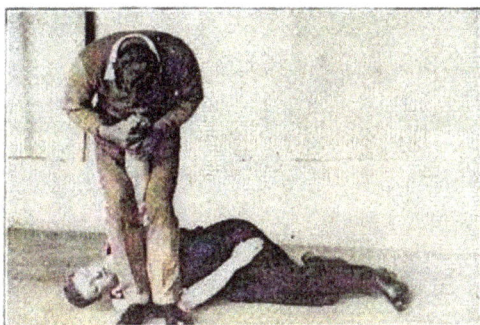

Fig. 120

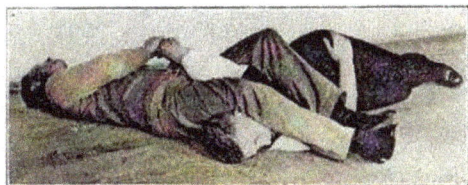

Fig. 121

No. 6.—ANKLE THROW.

1. Stand facing your opponent.
2. Seize both his arms above the elbows.
3. Pull downwards with your right hand and lift upwards with your left (this will pull the weight of his body on to his left leg); at the same time strike his left ankle with the sole of your right foot without bending your leg (Fig. 122).

Note.—The blow of your right foot on your opponent's left ankle should be made with sufficient force to sweep his legs from under him.

No. 6.—Ankle Throw.

Fig. 122

No. 7.—INSTEP THROW.

1. Stand facing your opponent.
2. Seize him under the armpits with both hands, your toes turned outwards, and pull him towards you (Fig. 123).
3. Sinking from the knees, fall backwards, simultaneously pulling upwards with your hands and kicking his legs backwards as in Fig. 124.
4. This will throw your opponent over your head (Fig. 125).

Caution.—It should be noted that the Instep Throw is a very dangerous throw. Should your opponent be unacquainted with the "art of falling" he will probably meet with serious injury.

No. 7.—Instep Throw.

FIG. 123

FIG. 124

FIG. 125

No. 8.—LEG OR SCISSOR THROW.

1. Stand on the right of your opponent (one to two feet away), facing in the same direction.

2. Seize the upper part of his right arm with your left hand (Fig. 126).

3. Jumping inwards, throw your left leg across the front of his legs and your right behind his knees (Fig. 127).

4. Almost simultaneously placing your right hand on the ground and turning your body to the rear, pulling him backwards by his right arm. This will bring him into the position shown in Fig. 128.

No. 8.—LEG OR SCISSOR THROW.

FIG. 126

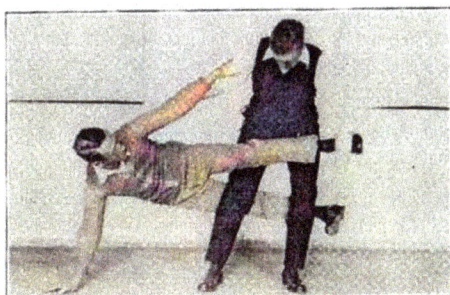

FIG. 127

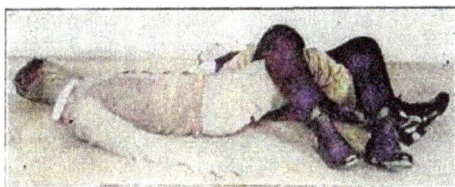

FIG. 128

93

No. 9.—Leg or Scissor Throw, with Leg Lock.

1. Having secured the throw as in Fig. 128, keep twisting your body towards your left, keep your legs
   straight and let go his right arm. This will turn
   your opponent over on to his stomach (Fig. 129).

2. Seize his right foot with your left hand and bend his
   leg from the knee, over your right leg (Fig. 130).

Note.—Should your opponent attempt to get up, force his right foot
downwards and in the opposite direction to that in which he is
trying to raise himself.

No. 9.—Leg or Scissor Throw, with Leg Lock.

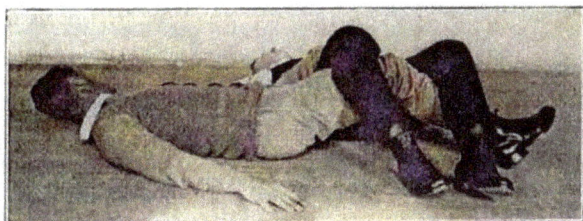

Fig. 128

Fig. 129

Fig. 130

EDGE OF THE HAND BLOWS.

It is not generally known that a person can hit with more force with the edge of the hand than with the clenched fist.

A person striking with his clenched fist distributes the force of the blow over a much larger surface than would be the case if he struck with the edge of his hand.

It stands to reason that a blow covering only one square inch of the body must be more painful than if it were distributed over four, providing that both blows are delivered with the same amount of force.

Further, an Edge of the Hand Blow, delivered in the manner shown in Fig. 131 ("Forearm Blow"), would break the forearm bone. This would be impossible with a blow from the clenched fist.

Note.—An "Edge of the Hand Blow" is given with the inner (*i.e.* little finger) edge of the palm, fingers straight and close together, thumb extended.

EDGE OF THE HAND BLOWS.

FOREARM

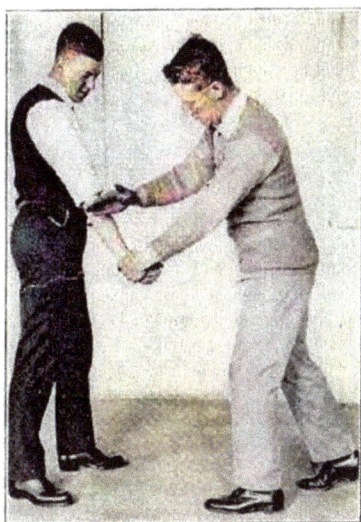

FIG. 131

97

FOREARM

WRIST

FIG. 181

FIG. 182

BICEPS

NECK

FIG. 183

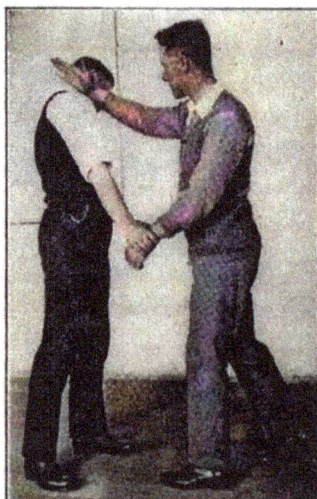

FIG. 184

EDGE OF THE HAND BLOWS

FACE	SHOULDER

FIG. 135

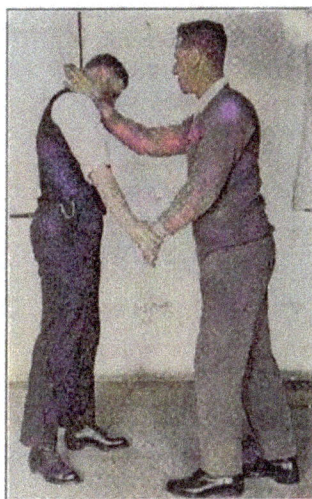

FIG. 136

NECK	NECK

FIG. 137

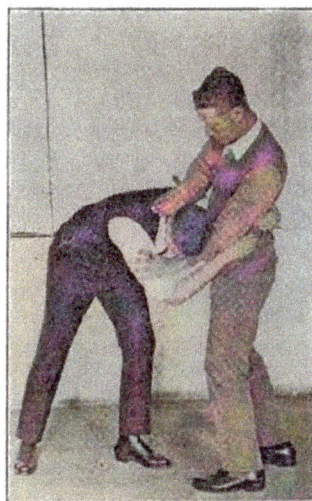

FIG. 138

THIGH

SHIN

FIG. 139

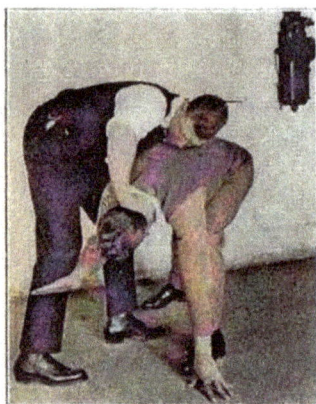

FIG. 140

LEG

WAIST

FIG. 141

FIG. 142

KIDNEY

FIG. 143

SPINE

FIG. 144

101

No. 1.—Use of the Baton, "Night Stick" or Club.

Police clubs are provided with a leather thong or cord so that they can be secured to the hand. This prevents them from being snatched away. It is, in consequence, very important that all policemen should know the correct manner in which this thong or cord should be used.

For instance, if the thong were securely fixed around the wrist, and the club seized, it would be very difficult for its user to free himself, and he could easily be thrown to the ground by it.

To prevent this, the club should be held in the following manner:

1. Pass your right thumb through the loop (Fig. 145).
2. Pass the thong over the back of your hand to the palm (Fig. 146).

Note.—The thong or cord should be of sufficient length (but on no account longer) so that the head of the club will be in the center of the palm of the hand. By keeping a firm grip, it is impossible for an assailant to snatch it away. But should the club be seized, all that is necessary is to release the hold on the handle and the thong will slip off the thumb.

The blow with the club should be given in the same manner as a blow with a hammer, the wrist must be free. If the club is held as in Fig. 147 the wrist is partly locked and the force of the blow is checked. The above applies equally to loaded hunting crops when used as weapons of defense.

USE OF BATON, "NIGHT STICK" OR CLUB

No. 1.—Use of the Baton, "Night Stick" or Club.

Fig. 145

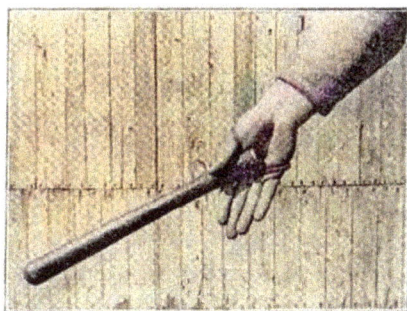

Fig. 146

Fig. 147

103

No. 2.—"Club Blow."

1. To bring your assailant to the ground, hit him on the shin bone below the knee-cap (Fig. 148). This is more effective than a head blow.

2. To make your assailant release his hold of any weapon with which he may be armed, hit him on either the forearm or wrist.

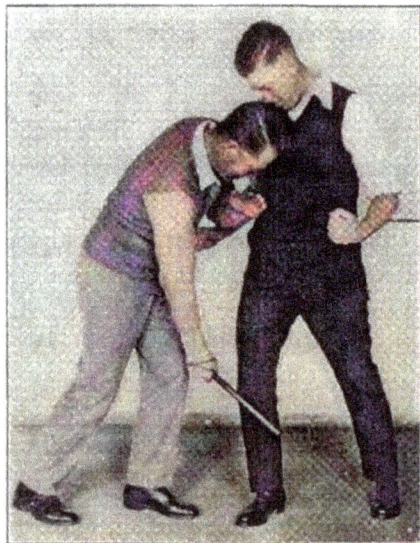

Fig. 148

No 3.—THE CLUB AS A PROTECTION.

To ward off a blow with a stick or similar weapon at your head:

1. Grasp the club with both hands near the ENDS, rush in as close as possible, taking the blow on the club (Fig. 149).

2. Release hold with your left hand and strike with club by a swinging blow at your assailant's shins. This will bring him to the ground.

Note.—It is to be noted that an assailant with a stick or other striking weapon can do little injury if you keep close to him.

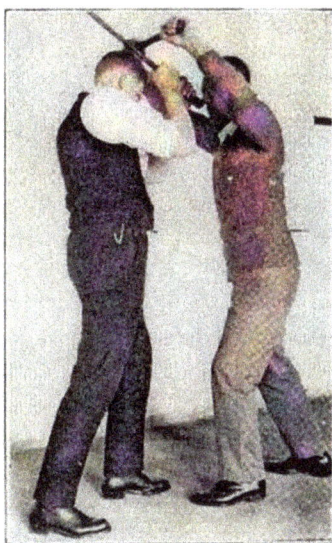

FIG. 149

No. 4.—THE CLUB USED AS HANDCUFFS.

Having thrown your opponent, as in Fig. 150. (Hand-cuff Hold, page 53).

1. Pass the thong over his right wrist.
2. Seize his left wrist and pass it through the loop of the thong.
3. Twist the club until the thong cuts into the wrists.
4. Keeping hold of the club with your right hand, stand up and assist your opponent to rise (Fig. 151).

No. 4.—The Club Used as Handcuffs.

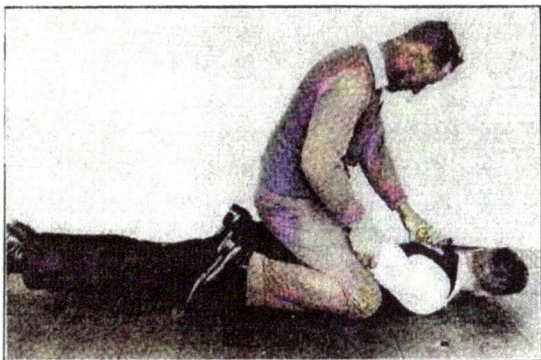

Fig. 150

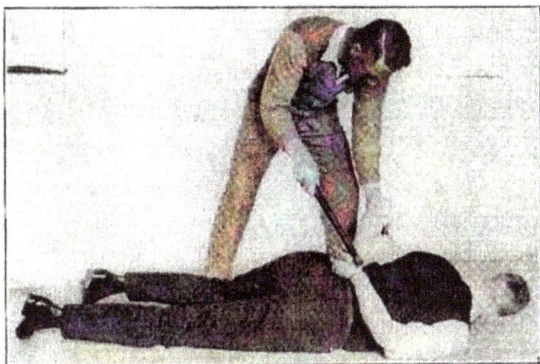

Fig. 151

107

No. 5.—Silk Cord v. Leather Thong.

It is recommended that a silk cord be used on police night sticks or clubs instead of a leather thong. The silk cord is much stronger and can be lengthened at will and used as a tourniquet in case of an accident (Fig. 152).

The cord should be of sufficient length (2-ft. 6-in.) to permit it being passed over any part of the thigh or arm, and should be secured to the club as in Fig. 153.

To shorten the cord to the correct length, so that the head of the club comes in the palm of the hand, make a number of "half hitches" and pass them over the head of the club (Fig. 154).

Fig. 152

108

No. 5.—Silk Cord v. Leather Thong.

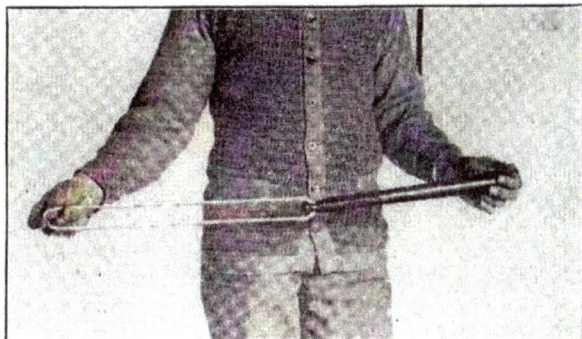

Fig. 153

Fig. 154

ATTACK AND DEFENCE WITH A WALKING STICK.

The art of usng a walking stick in attack or defence is not generally known, yet it is possible for anybody to master a very powerful man if the following instructions be carried out:

To bring your assailant to the ground, hit him on the shins, just below the knee-cap (Fig. 155), or jab him in the stomach with the point.

Note.—Never attempt to strike your assailant over the head, as this can be very easily guarded. In fact, it is almost impossible to strike a person over the head, if he is aware that you are about to do so. Further he would be sure to close with you, and the stick would prove a handicap in preventing you from securing an effective hold.

The best class of stick is a medium weight ash or a Malacca cane.

ATTACK AND DEFENCE WITH A WALKING STICK.

FIG. 155

111

No. 1.—Arm and Neck Hold, with-a Stick.

1. Holding your stick in the left hand, thumb to the left, stand level with your opponent on his right side, facing the same way.

2. Seize his right wrist with your right hand, back of your hand to the front, back of his hand downwards.

3. Raise his right arm with your right hand; at the same time pass the stick under the arm to the back of his neck (Fig. 156).

4. Pull downwards on his right arm and lift upwards with the stick (Fig. 157).

Note.—Care must be taken that the stick is above your opponent's right elbow, otherwise you cannot get any leverage on the arm.

No. 1.—Arm and Neck Hold, with a Stick.

Fig. 156

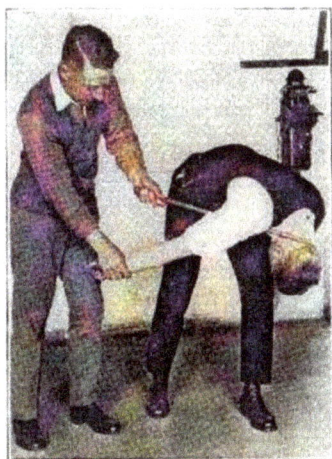

Fig. 157

No. 2.—Arm Hold, with a Stick.

1. Holding your stick in the left hand, thumb to the handle, stand level with your opponent on his right-hand side, facing the same way.
2. Seize his right wrist with your right hand, back of your hand to the front, back of his hand downwards.
3. Pass the stick under his right arm, above the elbow, to his chest (Fig. 158).
4. Push forward on the stick with your left hand and pull his right backwards with your right hand (Fig. 159).

No. 2.—Arm Hold, with a Stick.

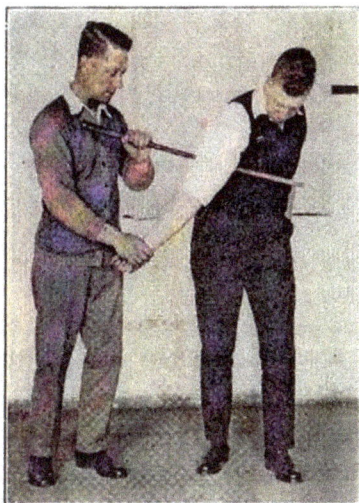

Fig. 158

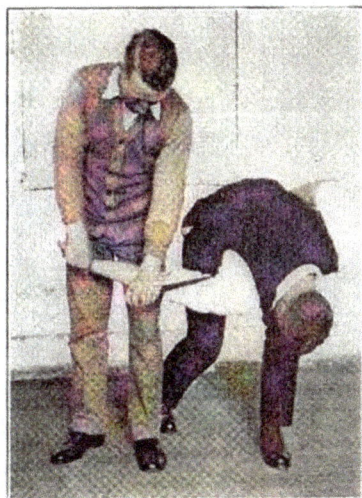

Fig. 159

No. 3.—BACK STRANGLE HOLD, WITH A STICK.

1. Holding your stick in the right hand, thumb towards the handle, stand at your opponent's back.
2. Place the stick around his neck, from his left-hand side (Fig. 160).
3. Pass your left hand over your right arm and seize the stick close up to your opponent's neck.
4. Force your forearms into the back of his neck, and pull the stick towards you (Fig. 161).

Note.—This is a very severe hold and extra care must be taken in practicing it, otherwise you will cause unnecessary pain.

No. 3.—Back Strangle Hold, with a Stick.

Fig. 160

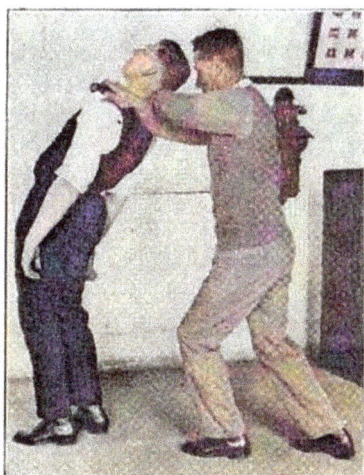

Fig. 161

117

No. 4.—CROTCH AND ARM HOLD, WITH A STICK.

1. Holding your stick in the left hand, thumb towards the handle, stand level with your opponent on his right side.

2. Pass the stick between his legs, seizing his right wrist with your right hand, back of your hand to the front, back of his hand downwards (Fig. 162).

3. Forcing the stick against the back of his left thigh, twist his wrist outwards and away from you with your right hand and pull it across your left leg, at the same time bringing the stick to the back of his right arm.

4. Holding his right arm straight, force downwards on the back of his right arm with the stick (Fig. 163).

No. 4.—Crotch and Arm Hold, with a Stick.

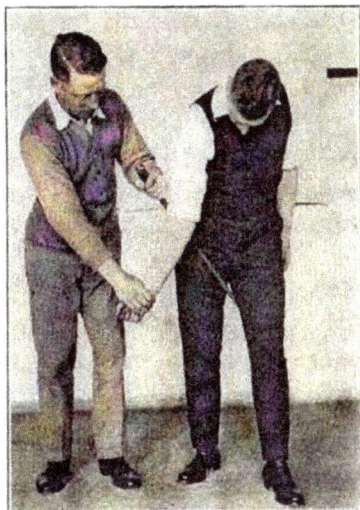

Fig. 162

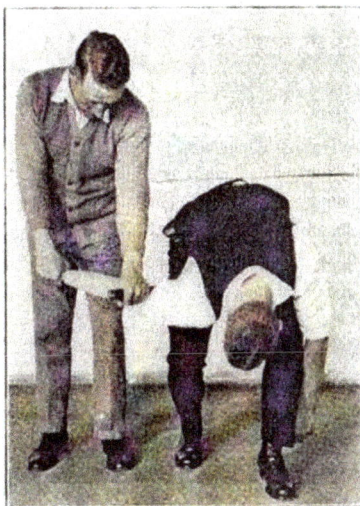

Fig. 163

119

No. 5.—NECK THROW, WITH A STICK.

1. Holding your stick in the right hand, stand level with your opponent on his right side.
2. Pass the stick across your opponent's throat, grasp the other end with your left hand close up to the neck, simultaneously stepping behind him (Fig. 164).
3. Bending your arms from the elbows towards you, jerk him backwards to the ground (Fig. 165).

Note.—This throw is very severe and like No. 3 Back Strangle Hold, page 116, extra care must be taken in practicing it.

No. 5.—Neck Throw, with a Stick.

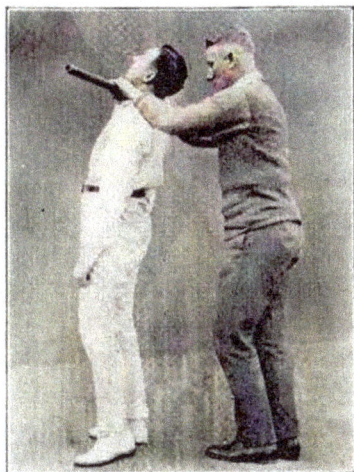

Fig. 164

Fig. 165

TYING AN EFFECTIVE KNOT.

Practice tying the following knot on a stick, pole or anything similar:

Take a piece of cord or silk rope about a quarter of an inch in diameter, and from 5 to 7 yards in length. This can be carried or tied around the waist under the jacket.

1. Pass the cord behind the pole with, the *Short* end of the cord to the left and the *Long* end to the right (Fig. 166).

2. Pass the *Long* end of the cord, in a loop, over the pole and through the loop held in the left hand, then pull down on the *Short* end with the right hand (Fig. 167).

3. Pass the *Short* end of the cord, in a loop, over the pole and through the loop held in the left hand (Fig. 167), which will form the knot shown in Fig. 168.

4. Holding the loop in the left hand, pull down on the *Long* end of the cord, pass the left hand through the loop and pull on both *Ends* of the cord (Fig. 169).

Note.—For the purpose of illustrating clearly, rope was used instead of cord.

TYING AN EFFECTIVE KNOT.

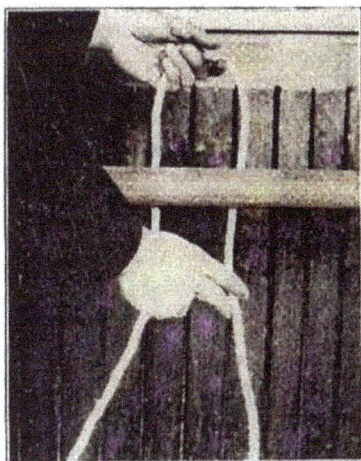

FIG. 166

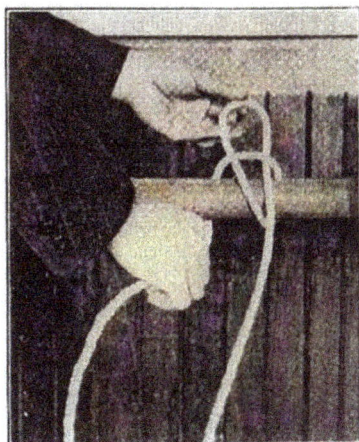

FIG. 167

FIG. 168

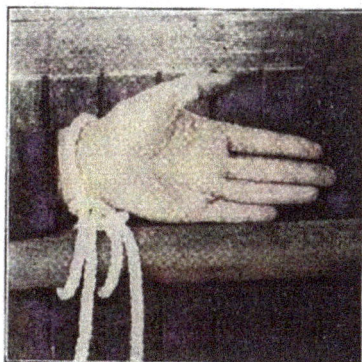

FIG. 169

TYING A PRISONER.

As is the case when using handcuffs, your prisoner is always more secure when his hands are fastened together behind his back: you would naturally compel him to precede you and you would then at once notice any attempt he might make to release his hands.

The knot shown on page 123 forms a very good substitute for a pair of handcuffs.

Tie the knot as shown in Fig. 170 on your prisoner's wrist, pass his other hand through the loop, held in the left hand and pull taut, then tie two half hitches to prevent slipping (Fig. 171).

TYING A PRISONER.

FIG. 170

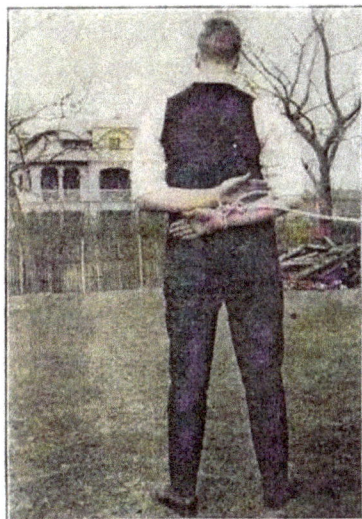

FIG. 171

TYING UP AN OPPONENT.

Should it be necessary that you have to leave your opponent without a guard, the following method of securing him will be found very effective:

Secure his hands as in Fig. 171, throw him on the ground, pass the cord around his neck, pass the end under his hands. Bend his left leg backwards and tie two half hitches round his ankle (Fig. 172).

Note.—If your prisoner keeps still he will not hurt himself, but the more he moves the greater the discomfort he will suffer.

TYING UP AN OPPONENT.

FIG. 171

FIG. 172

127

To Lift a Man on to His Feet from the Ground.

Your opponent lies on his stomach on the ground and refuses to stand up.

1. Stand to one side or over your opponent.
2. Seize him round the neck with both hands, your fingers pressing into his neck alongside the "Adam's apple" (Fig. 173).
3. Force the points of your thumb into the hollows under the lobe of the ears and lift upwards (Fig. 174).

To Lift a Man on to His Feet from the Ground.

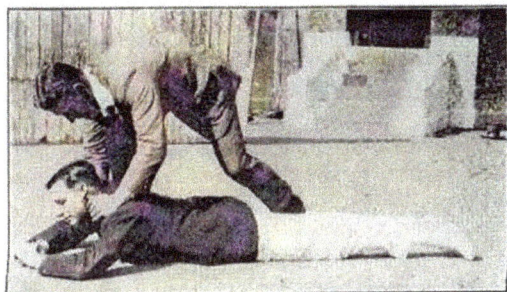

Fig. 173

Fig. 174

The Handkerchief or Glove as an Aid to Securing a Hold or Throw.

Under certain circumstances the pocket handkerchief is a great aid in securing an effective hold or throw, such as when a policeman is called into a building to eject a person.

Your opponent is standing and from all appearance is about to resist being put out of the building.

1. Speak to him quietly but firmly and ask him to leave, at the same time taking your handkerchief in your hand.

2. Suddenly throw the handkerchief in his face, simultaneously closing with him. This will take him off his guard and you should have no difficulty in applying one of the holds or throws demonstrated, in Figs. 57, 80, 100, 104, 116 and 122.

POLICE HOLD   STRANGLE HOLD

FIG. 57

FIG. 80

MISCELLANEOUS ADVICE

THE HANDKERCHIEF OR GLOVE AS AN AID TO SECURING A HOLD OR THROW.

HEAD HOLD

FIG. 100

WRIST THROW

FIG. 104

HIP THROW

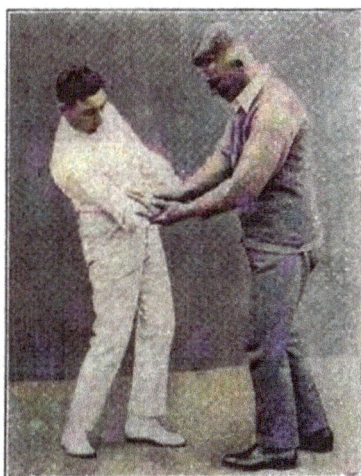

FIG. 116

ANKLE THROW

FIG. 122

How to Deal with an Assailant Following You at Night.

It gives rise to a very uncomfortable feeling to realize that you are being followed, especially if it should happen to be on a dark night and the road a lonely one. The best thing to do under these circumstances is to carry the war into the enemy's camp rather than to wait for him to attack you. If you turn on him it will prove such a surprise to your assailant that you will have little difficulty in securing an effective hold or throw.

Having become aware that you are being followed:

1. Shorten your pace and allow your assailant to come within eight or ten paces.
2. Without losing a pace, suddenly turn around and walk towards him.
3. Apply one of the holds or throws shown on pages 130 and 131.
4. Should your assailant be armed with a stick or other striking weapon, close with him. Providing this is done quickly it will be very difficult for him to do you any injury.
5. If there should be two assailants, and they attempt to close in on you (a very old dodge), suddenly "Chin Jab" them both (Fig. 175).

Note.—Providing you have taken the precaution of turning up your coat collar and have not missed a pace whilst turning, your assailant, still hearing your footsteps, will on a dark night not be aware that you are coming towards him, until you have actually closed upon him.

132

How to Deal with an Assailant Following You at Night.

Fig. 175

THE FARCE OF THE "FIREMAN'S LIFT."

(Raising and carrying an unconscious person, single-handed.)

It is not generally known that the method of picking up and carrying an unconscious person, commonly known as the "Fireman's Lift," which one sees demonstrated in nearly every book on First Aid, is an impossibility.

The instructions are usually as follows:

1. Turn the patient on to his face and then raise him to a kneeling position.
2. Place yourself under him, so that his stomach is on your right shoulder.
3. Pass your right arm between his thighs and behind his right thigh, grasping his right wrist with your right hand (Fig. 176).

To carry out the above, with a conscious subject, is easy enough, for the simple reason that when raised to a kneeling position he keeps his joints stiff. Were, however, the subject really unconscious he would not remain in a kneeling position, unless held there, but would collapse from the hips and fall sideways or forward (Fig. 177).

In addition, very few people, even when in a standing position, are strong enough to lift an unconscious body clear off the ground, and to attempt to do so from a kneeling position is an utter waste of time.

MISCELLANEOUS ADVICE

The Farce of the "Fireman's Lift."

Fig. 176

Fig. 177

MISCELLANEOUS ADVICE

THE ART OF FALLING

Japanese jiu-jitsu experts consider the art of falling correctly, *i. e.*, without hurting one's self, of more importance than the ability to secure an effective hold or trip, and it is owing to this that they are able to fall and be thrown about in competition in such a manner that, to a stranger, appears to be asking for a broken limb, yet they no sooner hit the ground than they are again on their feet.

The fact that falling backwards down a flight of stairs can be accomplished without the slightest injury by any one who has made a thorough study of this art, clearly demonstrates that a little practice at a few simple but very useful falls, etc., will well repay the student for his trouble.

Caution.—Students are warned that the fall, shown on pages 138 and 189 should first be practiced from the kneeling or crouching position as shown on the following pages.

The following is an extract from the *North China Daily News*, November 23, 1916.

THE LYCEUM THEATRE

"THE BREED OF THE TRESHAMS"

There was a gorgeous stage fight in the second act, with a stage fall downstairs by a man shot dead, such as we have never seen equalled.

From the *North China Daily News*, November 24, 1916.

Praise that is given unawares is the best praise of all, and in mentioning yesterday that the fall downstairs of a man shot dead was such as we have never seen equalled (referring to the second act of "The Breed of the Treshams" on Saturday night) the writer thought he was giving recognition to some good acting by a member of the Howitt-Phillips Company. The realistic fall of the dead man down a steep flight of stairs was done, not by an actor, but by a policeman, W. E. Fairbairn, the drill instructor of the Shanghai

136

Municipal Police, and although he had rehearsed the scene he had not rehearsed the actual fall. Such things come natural to policemen, especially to jiu-jitsu men. And beside Fairbairn, there were seven other Shanghai policemen in the show that night, so that the "guards" were real guards, with the result that the stage fight was as real as safety would allow.

SIDE FALL

FIG. 178

HAND SPRING

FIG. 179

"FLYING" DIVE

FIG. 180

STOMACH FALL

FIG. 181

CROUCH FALL

FIG. 182

FACE FALL

FIG. 183

No. 1.—"Rolling Dive."

(Kneeling Position.)

This must first be learnt in the following manner, and on no account must it be attempted from the standing position until the pupil is proficient, otherwise there is danger of injury to the head, neck and kidneys:

1. Kneel on the right knee, place the back of the right hand and forearm on the ground under the body (Fig. 184).
2. Place the left hand on the ground in front of the left shoulder, turning the head to the left-hand side (Fig. 185).
3. Throw yourself forward over the right shoulder on to your left side, bending the lower part of the left leg from the knee, towards the right-hand side, the right foot to be over the left leg and in the position shown in Fig. 186.

No. 1.—"Rolling Dive." (Kneeling Position.)

Fig. 184

Fig. 185

Fig. 186

No. 1.—"ROLLING DIVE."

(Crouching Position.)

When proficient from the kneeling position as demonstrated on page 141, it should be practiced from the crouching position as follows:

Bend forward from the waist, placing the back of the right hand on the ground, left hand and head to the left-hand side (Fig. 187). Then throw yourself forward over the right shoulder and carry on as from the kneeling position. Providing you have not forgotten to turn the head to the left-hand side and allowed the spine to bend when turning over, it should only be necessary to practice this dive from the crouching position a few times.

No. 1.—"ROLLING DIVE." (Crouching Position.)

FIG. 187

No. 1.—"ROLLING DIVE."

(Standing Position.)

1. Standing as in Fig. 188, turn the head to the left and throw yourself forward head-over-heels.
2. Fig. 189 shows the feet and hands ready to strike the ground a fraction of a second before the body reaches the position shown in Fig. 190.
3. Fig. 191 shows the position just before the completion of the "Dive."

Note.—All the above movements must be continuous, but should you wish to remain on the ground, hold your right foot as in Fig. 186, (page 141), which will prevent you from coming up on to the feet.

FIG. 188

No. 1.—"ROLLING DIVE." (Standing Position.)

FIG. 189

FIG. 190

FIG. 191

145

No. 2.—SIDE FALL.

This fall must first be practiced from the following position:

1. Crouch as in Fig. 192, throw yourself on to your right-hand side, striking the ground with the open palm of your right hand a moment before your body reaches the ground (Fig. 193), care being taken that the right arm is at an angle of 45 degrees from the body: this protects the elbow. At the same time bring the left foot over the right leg into the position shown in Fig. 194.

Note.—Placing the left foot in the above position turns the body on to the right side, with the results that kidneys and head are prevented from striking the ground. When proficient in the above it should be practiced from the standing position.

This fall is used when thrown by the "Hip Throw" and is also an old trick for a person wishing to fall himself, in order to get into a favourable position to throw his opponent. See Figs. 195 and 196, (page 149).

No. 2.—Side Fall.

Fig. 192

Fig. 193

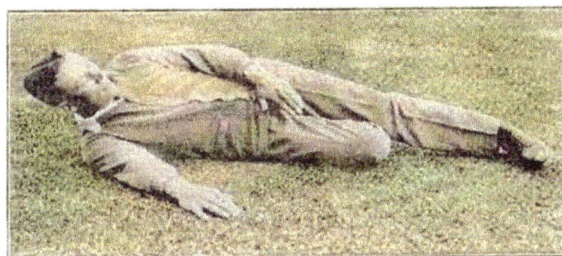

Fig. 194

147

No. 3.—Side Fall, with Throw and Leg Lock.

Your opponent having thrown you by the Hip Throw, and you are in the position shown in Fig. 195:

1. Turn over sharply on to the left side, pass your right leg around and to the back of his knees, placing your left leg over his feet at the instep (Fig. 196).
2. Twist your body sharply towards your right-hand side at the same time striking his feet backwards with your left leg and striking his legs forward with your right leg at the back of his knees. This will bring you into the position shown in Fig. 197.
3. Seize his right foot with your left hand and bend his right leg, from the knee, over your left leg. Apply pressure by twisting your body sharply towards your right-hand side, simultaneously forcing his right foot downwards (Fig. 198).

Note.—All the above movements must be continuous.

No. 3.—Side Fall, with Throw and Leg Lock.

Fig. 195

Fig. 196

Fig. 197

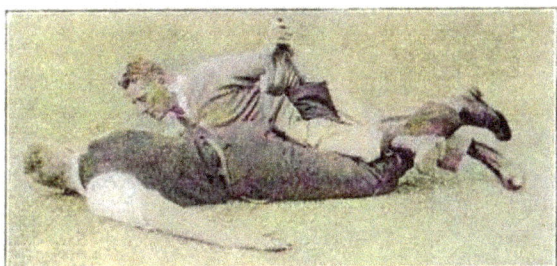

Fig. 198

149

No. 4.—FRONT FALL.

This fall must first be practiced from the following position:

1. Kneeling on the knees, hands and arms held slightly in advance of the body, palm of the hands to the front, with fingers and thumbs as shown in Fig. 199.
2. Fall forward on to the forearms and hands as shown in Fig. 200.

Caution.—At the moment the forearms and hands touch the ground, raise on to the toes, bringing the knees and stomach clear of the ground and allow the arms to bend forward from the elbows to take the shock of the fall. When proficient, practice from the standing position.

Note.—This fall is used when there is insufficient room to do a "Rolling Dive."

No. 4.—Front Fall.

Fig. 199

Fig. 200

No. 5.—Getting Up from the Ground.

Having fallen or been thrown, as in Fig. 201:

1. Turn your body sharply towards your left-hand side, stomach to the ground, raising by the help of the right forearm and right knee to the position shown in Fig. 202.

2. Pushing with both hands, force yourself into the position shown in Fig. 203 and then stand up.

Note.—All the above movements must be one continuous roll or twist of the body. Further, having arrived at the position shown in Fig. 203, and your opponent is behind you, and you want to face him, turn sharply on your left foot, backwards towards your left-hand side, when you will be in the position shown in Fig. 204.

Fig. 201

152

No. 5.—Getting Up from the Ground.

Fig. 202

Fig. 203

Fig. 204

153

No. 6.—Getting Up from the Ground (Backwards).

Having fallen or been thrown as in Fig. 205:

1. Place your right arm at an angle of 90 degrees from the body, back of hand on the ground, head towards your left shoulder (Fig. 206).
2. Raise your legs from the waist and shoot them over your right shoulder (Fig. 207).
3. Allow your right arm and hand to turn with your body; then by bending the right leg from the knee you will be in the position shown in Fig. 208.
4. Press on the ground with both hands and force yourself up to a standing position.

Fig. 205

No. 6.—Getting Up from the Ground (Backwards).

Fig. 206

Fig. 207

Fig. 208

COMBINATION THROW, WITH A "COAT STRANGLE."

You and your opponents have hold of each other's clothing, as in Fig. 209, and you are thrown by the "Hip Throw" (Fig. 210).

1. Do not release your hold, and whilst falling, pull downwards with your right hand and push with your left, simultaneously twisting your body towards your right-hand side; this will pull your opponent right over you and on to his back, as in Fig. 211.

2. Retaining your hold, pull yourself into the position shown in Fig. 212.

Continued on page 158

FIG. 209

COMBINATION THROW, WITH A "COAT STRANGLE."

FIG. 210

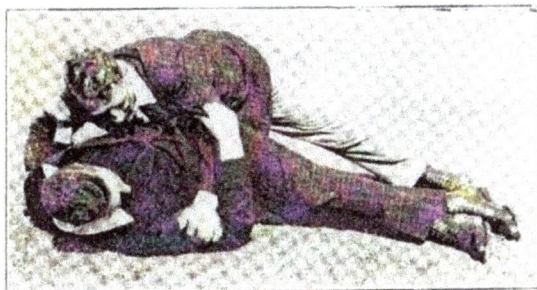

FIG. 211

FIG. 212

COMBINATION THROW, WITH A "COAT STRANGLE."

3. Release the hold with your right hand and seize the right lapel of his coat, the back of your hand inside the coat, the thumb outside, hand as near his neck as possible, at the same time passing your left hand under your right forearm and seize the left lapel of his coat as in Fig. 213.

4. Keeping a firm grip with both hands, apply pressure by forcing the little finger side of your right forearm under his chin and into his neck, squeezing his ribs with your thighs and forcing downwards with your body as in Fig. 214.

Note.—Should your opponent sink his chin into his chest in an attempt to prevent you from forcing your forearm into his neck, force your wrist bone on to the point of his chin and work it to and fro. This is very painful and will quickly make him raise his chin.

The alternative method is to fall sideways on to your back pulling your opponent over on top of you and in between your legs; you will then be in the position shown in Fig. 215. Lock your legs around his waist and apply pressure by pulling his neck towards you and forcing your forearm into his chin or neck, then shoot out your legs and squeeze his ribs (Fig. 216).

FIG. 213

COMBINATION THROW, WITH A "COAT STRANGLE."

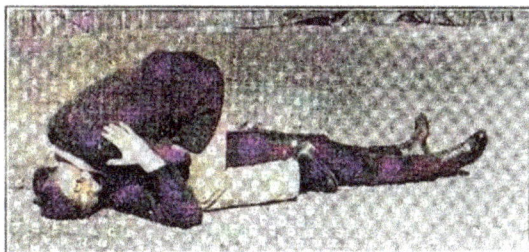

FIG. 214

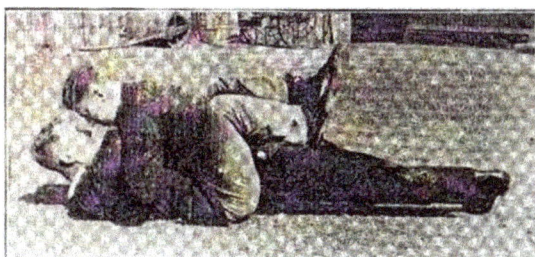

FIG. 215

FIG. 216

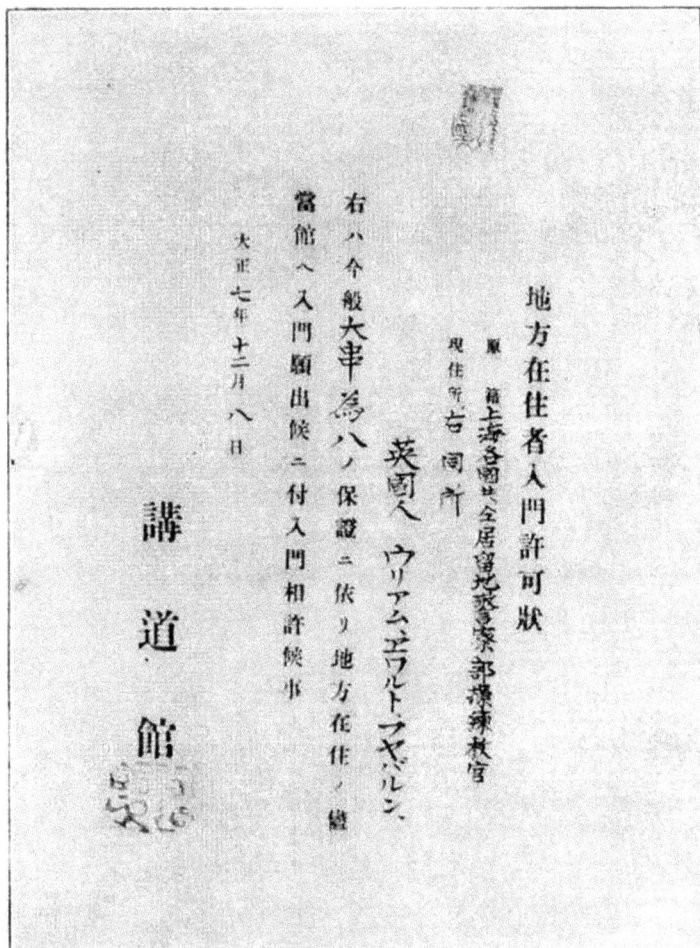

Translation of Certificate.

No. 217.　TOKIO JUI-JITSU UNIVERSITY (KODOKAN).
PERMISSION OF ENTRANCE.

The application for entrance of W. E. Fairbairn (resident in
Foreign Country), a Drill Officer of the Police Force, Shanghai
Municipal Council, having the guarantee of Tamehachi Ogushi, is
hereby permitted on the Eighth Day of the Twelfth Moon in the
Seventh Year of Taisho.　(8th December, 1918).

(KODOKAN SEAL).

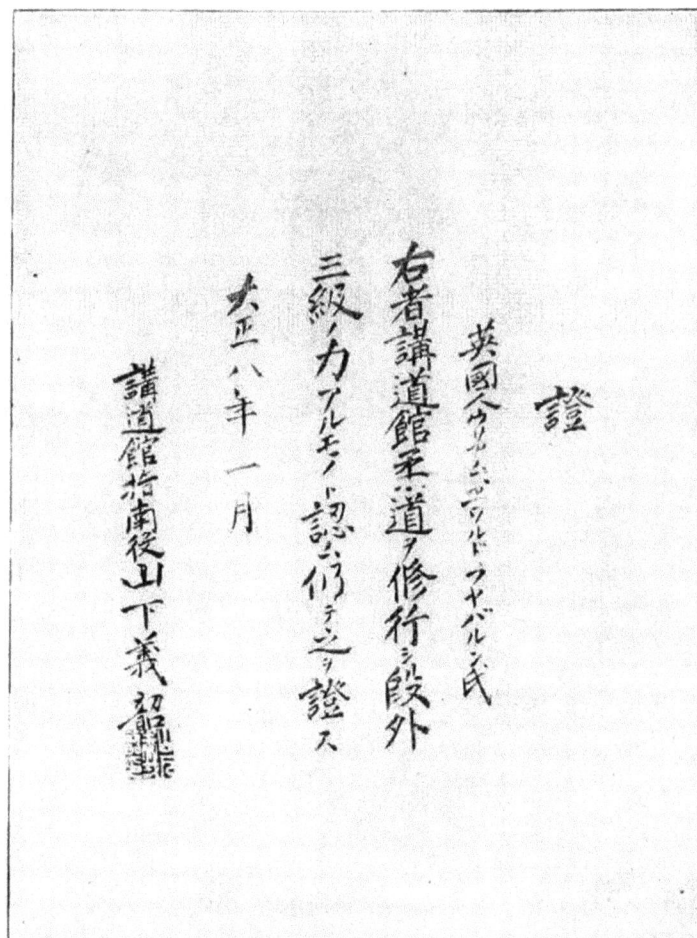

Translation of Certificate.

No. 218.　　　　　　BROWN BELT, 3RD DEGREE.

This is to certify that W. E. Fairbairn, British Subject, having satisfactorily acquired the art of Kodokan Judo (Jui-jitsu), is awarded the Brown Belt, 3rd Degree (San Kyu), of the Tokyo Jui-jitsu University.

　　　　　　　　(Sd.) Y. YAMASHITA, Lodokan Judo Instructor.
First Moon in the Eighth Year
　of Taisho (January, 1919).

　　　　　　　　　　　　　　　(KODOKAN SEAL).

161

之者也列ス向後益、研磨可有進歩ヲ見タリ依テ初段ニ修行ニ精力ヲ盡シ大ニ其ノ日本傳講道館柔道ノウリアム・エワルト、フヤバルン

大正十五年十二月十四日

講道館師範嘉納治五郎

Translation of Certificate.

No. 219.　　　　　BLACK BELT, 1ST DEGREE

This is to certify that William Ewart Fairbairn has this day been promoted to the rank of "First Degree" in the art of jui-jitsu in recognition of his progress due to energetic and zealous study and is hereby authorized to wear a Black Belt whilst engaged in the art.

This institution highly appreciates the manner in which W. E. Fairbairn has earned this honour and, while registering this record, hopes that, in future, he will merit further honours by continuous study and application.

(Signed & Sealed) JIGORO KANO,
President of the Kodokan
Jui-jitsu Institution, Tokyo.
14th day of the 12th moon of the 15th year of Taisho.
(December 14, 1926).

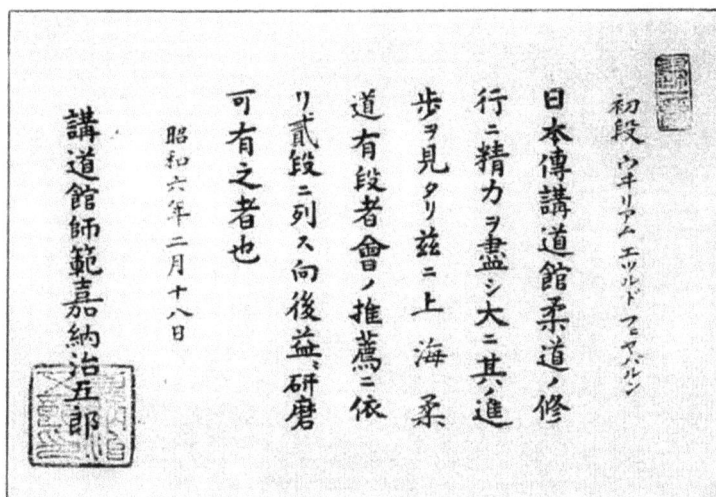

Translation of Certificate.

BLACK BELT, 2ND DEGREE

This is to certify that William Ewart Fairbairn who holds the rank of "First Degree" has this day been promoted to the rank of "Second Degree" in recognition of his further progress due to energetic and zealous study and by the recommendation of the Shanghai Jui-jitsu Association of Black Belt Holder.

This institution highly appreciates the manner in which W. E. Fairbairn has earned this honour and while registering this record, hopes that, in future, he will merit further honours by continuous study and application.

(Signed & Sealed) JIGORO KANO,
President of the Kodokan
Jui-jitsu Institution, Tokyo.

18th day of the 2nd moon of the 6th year of Showa.
(February 18, 1931).

Shanghai Municipal Council.

March   4,   1925.

The various forms of self-defence have in recent years become an essential factor in police training, and while practical instruction at the hands of an expert has been considered necessary in acquiring a working knowledge, this book, compiled by Inspector Fairbairn, will in a great measure enable the reader to teach himself. The admirable photographic illustrations, the brief and clear instructions, and the many orginal exercises described, are a great advance on anything yet published.

As the most up-to-date comprehensive work on defence against almost every form of attack, this book, called ''Defendu,'' should form a portion of the equipment of every police officer.

(sd.) K. J. McEUEN,

Commissioner of Police,
Shanghai,
China.

164

Shanghai Municipal Council.

_____March 4,_____ 19 25.

POLICE FORCE.
(COMMISSIONER'S OFFICE.)

TO CHIEF OFFICERS OF POLICE FORCES
AND OTHER INTERESTED PERSONS.

Sir,

This serves to introduce to you Inspector W.
Fairbairn, Drill Instructor of the Shanghai
Municipal Police who is proceeding home to England
on eight months furlough during which period it is
his intention to publish a book compiled by himself
on a system of self-defence known as ''Defendu.''

The methods contained in the book are
specially adopted for the use of policemen, are
simple and quite effective, as the bearer is quite
capable of demonstrating to any interested person.

I have much pleasure in recommending the book
to the careful consideration of the Chiefs of
Police Forces wishing to introduce an effective
method of defence against armed and other criminals.

Yours faithfully,

Commissioner of Police.

(1)

165